Circus techniques

juggling   equilibristics   vaulting

with photographs by
Judy Burgess

juggling

equilibristics

vaulting

Thomas Y. Crowell Company
New York / Established 1834

A Drama Book Specialists Publication

Circus techniques

BY HOVEY BURGESS

DESIGNED BY BETTY BINNS

Manufactured in the United States of America

Library of Congress Cataloging in Publication Data

Burgess, Hovey.
  Circus techniques.

    1. Acrobats and acrobatism.   2. Circus.   I. Title.
GV551.B87 1977   791.3'4   76-51205
ISBN 0-690-01463-5
ISBN 0-690-01464-3 (pbk.)

10 9 8 7 6 5 4 3 2 1

To the memory of
Buster Keaton and
Leonid Yengibarov

I have attempted to isolate certain universal and enduring principles of circus technique. Activities that meet my criteria for combining physicality with theatricality can usually—in their most elemental forms—be categorized under one of three designations: juggling, equilibristics or vaulting. Each of these is dealt with at three levels: humble beginnings (part one), pure forms (part two) and infinite possibilities (part three). The progression from one part to the next is generally toward a greater expenditure of time, space, energy and material. This approach to the subject is my own, but I hope it is one that will provide guidance in an area that is fraught with gross misconceptions, real dangers and Sisyphean demands. The concepts put forth here have been developed during a decade of practical teaching experience and twice as many years of performance, practice, observation and study. It is beyond the scope of this book to cover all the permutations of circus technique, but the basic principles can be seen in all kinds of situations, both in the performing arts and in everyday life.

It was not without a great deal of direct help that the manuscript for this book was prepared. Jane Herrmann, for two years my graduate assistant, spent long hours executing circus techniques with me in front of a camera. Behind the camera was Judy Burgess, my wife, who took the photographs. At my side preparing the text was John Towsen. As model, photographer and editor, these three—all former students—have had such input into this book as to make it as much their creation as mine. New York University provided me with time to work on the manuscript and space in which to shoot the photographs. Lexington Labs, Inc. processed an enormous amount of film and printed many enlargements in a very short period of time; Phil Pessoni of that firm was especially kind. Former students Cecil MacKinnon and David Stoudnour modeled for some of the photographs in chapters four, eight and nine. Lynda Wolfson of Hank Meyer Associates, Inc. provided the first photograph in chapter one. Diane L. Goodman typed the final manuscript.

Countless performers, teachers, colleagues, students and others have contributed to my circus education and therefore indirectly to this book. I am grateful to them all and hope they will understand the impossibility of thanking them all here. The following list of a dozen is merely representative of the kind of generosity to which I have been heir. Eloise Berchtold, trainer of wild animals, taught me to splice rope and instructed me in the basics of animal psychology and nonverbal communication. Dimitri, musician-juggler-acrobat-mime-clown, and Gunda, his wife, shared with me and my wife many moments of joy and mutual understanding. Ad Gilbert, director of the Sarasota High School Sailor Circus and later the Florida State University Flying High Circus, taught me to catch on the flying trapeze. Jack Haskin, founding director of the Florida State University Flying High Circus, expanded my appreciation of circus techniques. Theodore Hoffman, founding director of the Theatre Program of New York University's School of the Arts, and John Houseman, founding director of the Drama

Preface

Division of the Juilliard School, both gave me the opportunity to participate in the initial implementation of recent and exciting concepts of actor training. The late Harry H. Lind, a founding member of the International Jugglers' Association, designed and manufactured great juggling clubs and shared invaluable tips with me on how to pass them. Bobby May, the best club juggler the world has ever known, recounted for me the impact of seeing Rastelli perform. The late Joe Price made acrobatics comprehensible to me. Raymond Toole-Stott, compiler of the four-volume *Circus and Allied Arts: A World Bibliography, 1500-1970*, shared with me his collection of circus books. Alexander M. Voloshin, director of the Moscow Circus School since 1950, opened to me the doors of the oldest circus school in the world; currently called Gosudarstvennoe Uchilische Tsirkovogo i Estradnogo Iskusstva, it was established in 1926.

Finally I would like to thank my parents who endured much anxiety and suffering over what must have seemed at first a capricious and clandestine affair—my love for the circus. Had it not been for them, however, I doubt that my earliest memories would be of going to the circus. Indeed, it was my father who showed me how to juggle three balls—my mother who showed me how to walk on stilts.

H. B.

New York University
Easter. 1976

Contents

juggling

equilibristics

vaulting

Part two

Pure forms

Part three

Infinite possibilities

Appendix

Part one

Humble beginnings

In balance juggling, the performer supports an inanimate object in a vertical position using a single point of contact. The performer might even be a California sea lion (*Zalophus californianos*), famous for its ability to balance a ball or other objects on its nose (photo 1.1). Balance juggling is a fairly easy, familiar and basic form of juggling, but one that can also be developed to a high degree of difficulty and proficiency. It is basic because it has a wide application to more advanced circus skills, such as inverted equilibristics (chapter two), toss juggling (chapter four), stack equilibristics (chapter five), gyroscopic juggling (chapter seven) and even certain forms of rigging equilibristics (chapter eight). It is simple and accessible to all because it does not require any special equipment, setting or supervision to get started.

First lesson

The first lesson that I give in circus techniques almost invariably consists of balance juggling. Most students can recall having balanced objects at one time or another. Despite apprehensions and fears to the contrary, they find that they are beginning with something that is neither unfamiliar nor frightening. Since it is the first class meeting, many of the students show up in street clothes. I prefer that they wear sweat pants and a comfortable top of their own choosing and go barefooted. Since balance juggling does not require great freedom of movement and is not likely to ruin good clothing, we can get started right away. I have each student—one at a time—balance a cue stick. On many oc-

Balance juggling

casions I have used brooms, mop handles or other similar objects instead. While each student is concentrating on balancing the cue stick, I concentrate on learning his or her name and the other students observe a series of demonstrations, not on how to defy the law of gravity, but on how to work effectively within its limitations.

Balancing a cue stick

The thinner, lighter end of the cue stick is placed on the center of the flat, open palm of your hand while your eyes are focused on the top of the thicker, heavier end. As soon as the stick is vertical, release it into the custody of the balancing hand. Do not remove your gaze from the top of the stick. Try not to let the top move, but maneuver the base so that it remains, on the average, directly beneath the stick's center of gravity. With practice, you should become more skilled. You should be able to sustain the balance for longer periods of time with less perceptible movement and more awareness and control (photo 1.2). An industrial firm has recently designed an "electronic juggler" which uses a scanning device to keep a three-foot (91.44 cm) steel rod balanced on a supporting plate.

If you find balancing a stick particularly difficult, or if you do not improve with practice, checking yourself against the following points may prove helpful. Make sure that you are looking at the top of the stick, and not halfway up the stick or at your hand. Try not to waste too much of your energy and concentration preparing to catch the cue stick

PHOTO 1.1   Photo courtesy of the Miami Seaquarium.

PHOTO 1.2

PHOTO 1.3

PHOTO 1.4

should it fall. This preoccupation is usually manifested either by curving the fingers upward or by keeping the other hand very close to the stick so that the stick can be caught if and when it falls. In terms of theatricality, bending the fingers upward looks like cheating, even if they are not helping control the stick. If you tend to be overprotective with the other hand, try putting it behind your back. If you can direct all your energy to the task at hand and approach it with greater confidence, you are more certain to improve.

It is possible to balance a stick by stepping in the direction of its fall or by extending your arm in that direction. Be careful, however, that you do not overcompensate by using both methods simultaneously. If the stick is falling, lowering the hand may help a little, but raising the hand will only accelerate the fall.

When possible, make the base of the stick sway from side to side (photo 1.3) rather than forward and backward. This is more comfortable because your view of the stick's movement is not foreshortened and a side-to-side movement is less liable to upset the balance of your own body. Be sure to keep the hand fairly low and close to the body. Maintain a narrow stance, as this facilitates weight-shifting and effective footwork. Finally, try to be as relaxed as possible.

Generally a long pole is easier to balance than a short one. Before we can make an adjustment at the bottom of the pole, we must first perceive the movement taking place at the top. This movement is perceived in units of length but it affects the balance in direct

proportion to the number of degrees it leans over from its vertical position. To lose its stability, a nine-foot (2.74 m) pole would have to stray twice as far from the vertical axis than would a four-and-a-half-foot (1.37 m) cue stick. Therefore, your perception of movement occurs quicker and can be dealt with sooner when you are balancing a longer object. In theatrical terms, you may easily impress an unsophisticated audience by balancing a very long stick, but in physical terms you accomplish more when you attempt to balance progressively shorter sticks. As with all circus techniques, the greater your physical skills, the more options you will ultimately have theatrically.

You will also find it easier to balance an object when its heavier end is at the top, which is what we did with the cue stick. The explanation for this has to do with the object's center of gravity. It is useful to understand the concept of center of gravity because it plays a crucial role in many of the other techniques covered in this book. The center of gravity is the point around which an object's weight is evenly distributed or balanced. An object of consistent thickness and density would have its center of gravity at its geometrical center. A cue stick's center of gravity can be determined by locating its horizontal balance point (photo 1.4).

A nine-foot (2.74 m) pole with its center of gravity three feet (91 cm) from the top will have the "feel" of a twelve-foot (3.66 m) pole. If we reverse the pole so the center of gravity is three feet from the bottom, it will then have the "feel" of a six-foot (1.83 m) pole. This is why a stick is easier to balance if the heavier end is up, for this is much the same as balancing a longer object. In a perch pole act (chapter five), one performer (the understander) balances a long pole with his partner (the top-mounter) at the top of it. The top-mounter usually climbs up and slides down quickly, but—because the pole is most stable when the heavier end is up—he can take his time at the top.

Exploring the body

If you are right-handed, it is more than likely that you balanced the cue stick on your right hand, or vice versa if you are left-handed. In terms of circus technique, however, it would be self-limiting to learn skills with only one-half of your body. In fact, a certain degree of ambidexterity will be essential to almost all circus skills, particularly toss juggling (chapter four). You also can (and should) balance objects on other parts of your body. You need not take it for granted that one part of your body is somehow inherently superior to another part.

This dependence on certain parts of the body and neglect of others is very much a result of social attitudes that have prevailed in the West for thousands of years. The ingrained belief that right is better than left, upper better than lower, and front better than back, goes all the way back to Aristotle, who found this all very natural:

The dimensions by which animals are naturally bounded are six in number, namely superior and inferior, front and back, and also right and left. . . .Man more than any other animal has his left

limbs detached, because of all animals he is most in accord with nature, and the right is naturally better than the left and separated from it. . . .And since the right is differentiated, it is only reasonable that the left is less easily set in motion and most detached in man. Moreover, the other principles, the superior and the front, are in man most in accord with nature and most differentiated. . . .The superior is more honorable than the inferior, and the front than the back, and the right than the left.*

You can begin overcoming these prejudices with your work in this chapter. My method is to begin with the so-called good hand, but then soon move on to the other hand (photo 1.5). Having overcome the prejudice of right over left, we then move down to the inferior, learning to balance the cue stick on each foot (photo 1.6). Balancing an object on your foot can also be more difficult because you have to balance all your body's weight on the other foot. Therefore, any movement by the raised foot should ideally take place in a flat plane in front of you, using a side-to-side motion. Moving this foot forward and backward might cause you to lose your own balance because the weight of your body will be rocking back and forth between the toe and heel of your other foot. Do not forget to look at the top of the stick.

The next closest thing to an extremity is your chin, as it has a degree of mobility that the other parts of your head lack. When the base of the object is placed on your chin, the frequent result is a certain distortion of perception. The tendency is to concentrate on

*Aristotle, *Progression of Animals*, trans. by Edward Seymour Forster (Cambridge: Harvard University Press, 1937)

PHOTO 1.5

PHOTO 1.6

making your neck comfortable and to simply sight along the stick. You may perceive the stick as being straight, but being straight is not the same as being vertical. The sense of verticality is often lost when you tip your head back. To get some idea of it, place your chin against a wall and look up. The angle of the wall as you perceive it is the angle at which the stick can be balanced. This is similar to the optical illusion you experience when you stand at the base of a tall building and look up: The building looks as if it is about to fall over on you.

As with balancing on the hand or foot, the base of the stick must be maneuvered so as to keep it beneath the stick's center of gravity. This movement is usually achieved by means of footwork: You should be able to take a step in any direction. The head is bent backward, but the spine should be vertical and the knees slightly bent (photo 1.7).

The most common mistake is to try to control the stick by changing the angle of the head. This only makes things worse. The head must move in a horizontal plane, just as your hand moves in a horizontal plane when it is doing the balancing. You should not tip your head to another angle any more than you would tip your hand in order to maintain the balance.

Once you have balanced objects on these five extremities, you should be ready to explore the rest of your body. You will find that generally your body has less articulation in its central area than on its extremities. It may be easier to balance something on your limbs because they are capable of more movement, but it is more meaningful in terms of body awareness to be able to balance ob-

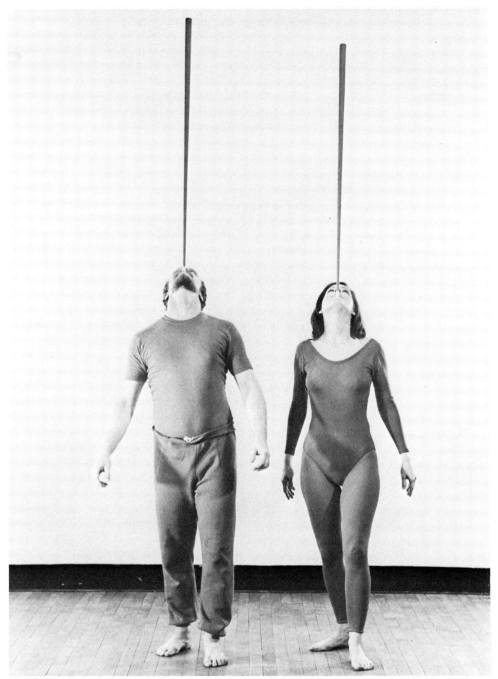

PHOTO 1.7

jects more centrally. First you might move the object up the arm a few inches at a time, gradually progressing to more difficult spots on the body, such as the knee, shoulder or hip (photos 1.8-1.11). In addition to the chin, other areas on the head also make useful places on which to balance objects. The forehead, the tip or bridge of the nose and the ear are all good spots (photos 1.12-1.15). However, heavy objects should not be balanced on the nose or ear because they might damage the cartilage. You will also probably discover that you cannot use the top or back of your head for balancing because you will not be able to see the top of the object.

The possibilities are practically unlimited and, if we are to believe certain erotic artworks, this even includes phallic balancing. A fifth century B.C. red-figured Greek psykter by Duris in the British Museum shows an actor in a satyr play balancing a kylix on an artificial phallus such as was commonly worn in satyr plays. Phallic balancing reappears in the eighteenth and nineteenth century Japanese scroll paintings of Jichosai and Shufu Kyosai as well as in the work of the pre-Victorian caricaturist, Thomas Rowlandson. These paintings may be more fanciful than documentary, but they certainly are imaginative.

Changing support

If you can balance a cue stick on the palm of your hand and on the back of your hand, you should be able to toss it up and switch the support from one side of the hand to the other. Keep your eyes focused on the top of

PHOTO 1.8

PHOTO 1.10

PHOTO 1.9

PHOTO 1.11

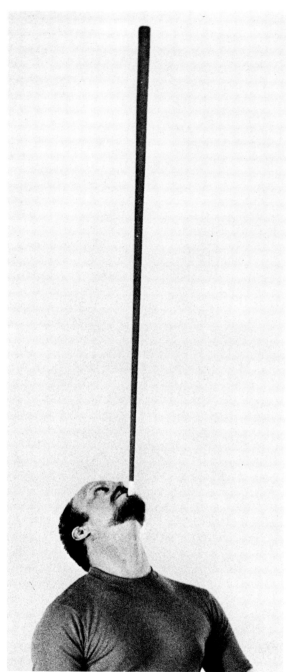

PHOTO 1.12

PHOTO 1.13

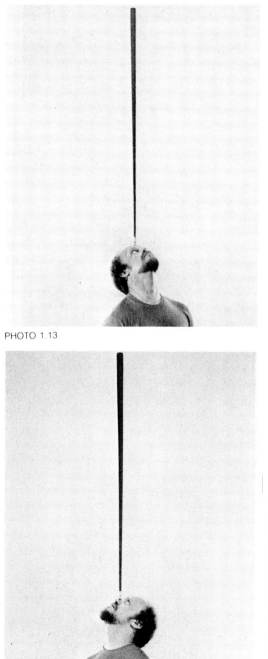

PHOTO 1.14

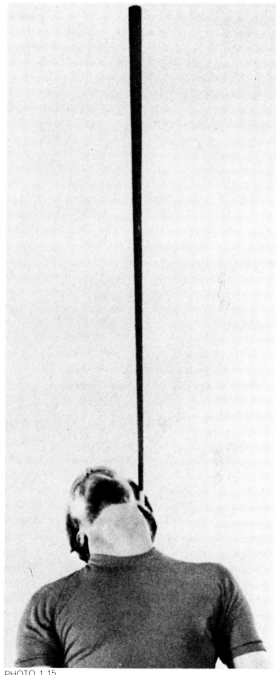

PHOTO 1.15

the stick and only toss it a few inches above the hand, all the time endeavoring to keep the stick as vertical as possible.

It is also quite easy to throw the cue stick from palm to palm. First bring the balancing hand in front of the center of your body (photo 1.16a). Now toss the stick straight up—a couple of inches is sufficient—but still keep your eyes focused on the top (photo 1.16b). Now quickly catch the stick on the (flat) palm of your other hand (photo 1.16c). You do not actually throw the stick across to the other hand. It stays on the same vertical axis and you simply switch supports. This technique could also be used to "throw" a balanced cue stick to a partner. More difficult variations may suggest themselves.

In the motion picture *The Old Fashioned Way* (Paramount, 1934), W. C. Fields (as the Great McGonigle) balanced a stick on his foot and then kicked it upward, catching it in a balance on the same foot after it had made a half-rotation. He then repeated the trick, this time catching it on his other foot.

Basic principles

Although I use a cue stick for the initial learning experience, the same basic principles can be applied to other kinds of objects. A baseball bat, rake, broom or stilt would all be further examples of "one-dimensional" (or linear) objects. "Two-dimensional" objects, such as a rectangular board or picture frame, can be balanced along their longest axis (a diagonal) or along a line that divides the rectangle lengthwise down the middle. Circular "two-dimensional" objects such as plates,

PHOTO 1.16c

PHOTO 1.16a

PHOTO 1.16b

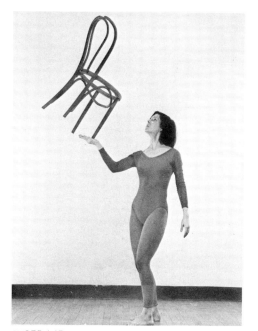

PHOTO 1.17

rings and hoops can be balanced along any diameter. "Three-dimensional" objects can be balanced along an imaginary line that cuts diagonally through the object, connecting two opposite, maximally distant corners. A chair, for example, might be balanced on one of its front legs (photo 1.17) or upside-down on its back (photo 1.18).

These basic principles will also have a wide application to many other circus techniques, and a thorough understanding of this section should broaden your whole approach to circus performing. More complicated variations on balance juggling follow but, as always, you are encouraged to invent your own as much as possible.

Object upon object

It is possible to stack objects together and then balance them as if they were a single object. You can, for example, balance more than just one chair on your chin. If the seats are removed from additional chairs so that they can be hooked over the legs of one another, you can create a pyramid of chairs by adding an equal number of chairs to each side of the bottom chair. You could balance three, five or even more chairs in this manner (photos 1.19 and 1.20). You must be able to sustain the total weight of all the chairs, but as far as the balance is concerned the added chairs cancel each other out. You can also balance one object on another by using one of the objects as an extension of your body. A common example of this would be to hold a stick in your hand and then balance another object on the end of it.

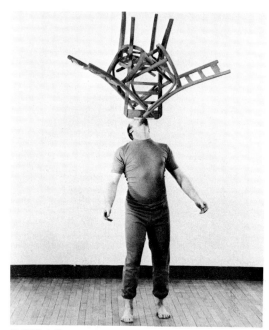

PHOTO 1.19

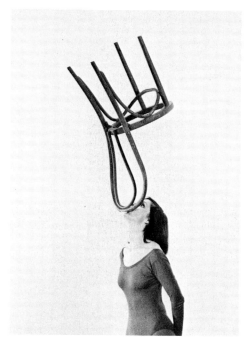

PHOTO 1.18

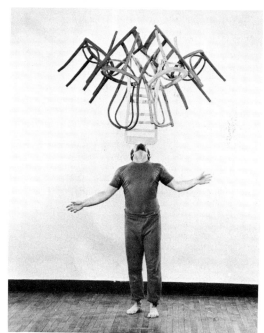

PHOTO 1.20

Controlled loss of balance

The controlled loss of balance, however accidental it might appear, offers possibilities for surprise that are often made use of by clowns. A peacock feather can be balanced on the tip of your nose (photo 1.21) very much like any other one-dimensional object, but it also has certain aerodynamic possibilities because of its weight and structure. If it is allowed to fall forward it will fall slowly. If you walk forward when it is at about a forty-five degree angle, you will create a slight breeze which can be utilized to maintain the angle of the feather (photo 1.22). If you walk a bit faster, you can walk the feather right back up to a vertical balance. If the air is calm, it is possible to keep the feather on your nose at an impossible-looking, almost horizontal angle by slowly walking forward. In order to keep the end of the feather from going in your eye, avoid tipping your head back too far or making sudden movements.

A ring, such as is used for ring juggling (chapter four) or eccentric spinning (chapter seven), can also be balanced across the bridge of your nose. If you allow it to fall backward, it will fall down around your neck. Do the same thing with the brim of a hat with the opening of the crown to the back and it will land on your head.

Sometimes a knockabout clown balances the back of a chair on his chin and then "takes a bow"; of course the chair falls off his chin and the seat of the chair hits him on the top of the head. The safest way to do this is to use a light chair with a heavily padded

PHOTO 1.21

PHOTO 1.22

seat or to hit the seat of the chair with the palm of your hand so as to break its fall and at the same time simulate the sound of its "hitting your head."

By far the most effective use of the controlled loss of balance that I have ever seen was at the Moscow Circus on my first trip to Moscow in 1970. It was performed by the late Armenian clown, Leonid Yengibarov (1935-1972) who, unfortunately, never made a tour of the West. Between two numbers he took one of the birch brooms used by the prop men to sweep the ring. He pulled the bundle of birch twigs off and tossed them aside. He hung his hat on the broom handle, draped his vest and scarf over the hat and placed his cane on top of them. He then balanced the whole assemblage on his forehead (photo 1.23). Suddenly he upset the balance. The broomstick fell on the floor, but the vest fell over his arms onto his back, the scarf fell around his neck, the hat fell on his head and the cane landed in his hand.

Simultaneous balances

You will probably find it very difficult to simultaneously balance two or more independent objects on different parts of your body. The simplest example of this would be to balance a cue stick on the palm of each hand, but even this is very difficult. Your cone of vision must include both objects, so your actual focus will be on an imaginary point between the tops of the two sticks. It is best to maintain just slightly less than shoulder-distance between the two sticks. In order to balance both sticks I find that I have

PHOTO 1.23

to balance one stick while I balance and control the other. Usually I have more control with my right hand, so if the top of the stick in my left hand moves forward, I deliberately cause the top of the stick in my right hand to do the same thing. I try to maintain the distance between the tops of the two sticks while keeping both sticks parallel. The hand that has the most control is usually compensating for the other hand. To start, I hold the cue sticks in the palms of my hands, gripping them with my fingers. When the sticks are parallel and the proper distance apart, I instantly open both hands and begin balancing (photo 1.24).

In 1968 I saw Bruski with the Hetzler Circus simultaneously balance four sticks surmounted with balls on his head, each hand and one foot while balanced on a high unicycle (chapter five). Perhaps only a person with balancing experience could appreciate the dynamic difficulty of such a static-looking trick.

Antithesis: the set

There is another kind of object balancing, called a set, which is quite different from balancing a cue stick. It is mentioned here as an exception to the principles set forth in this chapter. If you balanced a book on your head to improve your posture you would be performing a set (photo 1.25). The object's center of gravity is nearly at its base, and not high up as with the cue stick. It is not the same kind of balancing because you should not move the base in order to maintain the balance. In fact, you should keep the support

PHOTO 1.24

PHOTO 1.25

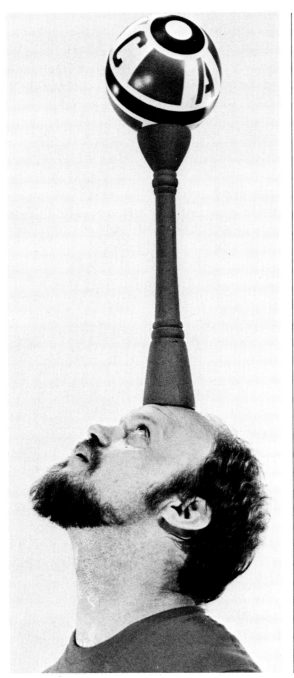

as still and horizontal as possible. You can balance a glass of liquid on the back of your hand or on your forehead if you are steady enough. You are simply taking the place of a flat surface, such as a table. Similarly, jugglers sometimes use a bottom-heavy pedestal to "balance" a light ball (photo 1.26). The lower section of the pedestal is lead-filled and shaped to accommodate the top of the juggler's head, the top section is hollow and shaped to accommodate a light ball.

PHOTO 1.26

In inverted equilibristics, the performer assumes various upside-down positions and maintains balance there. Inverted equilibristics includes much of what is traditionally known as hand balancing. As in chapter one, the performer might be a California sea lion which has been taught to balance on its front flippers or even to do a one-flipper stand. Even the African elephant (*Loxodonta africana*), largest of land mammals, and the Indian elephant (*Elephas maximus*) have been taught to balance on a single front leg. The little spotted skunk *(Spilogale putorius)* of the southwestern United States and Mexico does "handstands" (photo 2.1) and even runs balanced on its front paws, as recorded in *The Living Desert* (Walt Disney Productions, 1953). Inverted equilibristics requires no special equipment and affords excellent preparation for stack equilibristics (chapter five), tumble vaulting (chapter six) and most rigging equilibristics (chapter eight).

Squat headstand

The squat headstand is the most basic example of inverted equilibristics. With its broad base and low center of gravity it is roughly analagous to the set (chapter one). In general you will find that these positions become more difficult as you raise your center of gravity and/or reduce the base of support. The squat headstand is probably the most accessible balance for everyone and is a good preparation for the fully extended headstand. To begin, the hands and head are placed on a mat, rug or soft ground so as to form an equilateral triangle, the points of

2

Inverted equilibristics

which are shoulder-distance apart (photo 2.2a). Place the knees on the elbows and let the feet come off the floor (photo 2.2b). This is the squat headstand position (photo 2.2c).

Make sure you do not put your hands in a straight line with your head. You need a tripod foundation. Your center of gravity must be over the triangle in order to balance yourself. Anything other than an equilateral triangle will reduce your chances for success. The forearms should be perpendicular to the floor and the fingers should be pointing forward. The top of the head should support its share of the weight in a position that is comfortable for the neck. In the beginning, balance only for brief intervals and keep breathing so as to avoid dizziness.

Headstand

It is possible to go from the squat headstand to a fully extended headstand simply by lifting the hips and legs, with control, so that your center of gravity remains over the triangular base. From the squat headstand, the pelvis is brought to a position above the head while the knees come off the elbows and the legs are brought together (photo 2.3a). The legs are slowly raised with the knees still bent (photo 2.3b). Once the thighs are horizontal, the legs are straightened vertically over the body (photo 2.3c). This is the straight headstand position (photo 2.3d).

Try to maintain control even if you cannot extend fully on the first attempts. Do not kick up fast, but practice slowly going as far up as you can and back down again with control. In this way you can develop the strength

PHOTO 2.1

PHOTO 2.2a

PHOTO 2.2b

PHOTO 2.2c

PHOTO 2.3a

PHOTO 2.3b

PHOTO 2.3c

PHOTO 2.3d

and balance needed to do a fully extended headstand. If you lose the balance forward, tuck your head under, push with your hands and roll out of the headstand tucked in a ball. This is, in fact, a variation on the forward roll (chapter six). If you lose the balance to the back, you can simply bend your knees and flex your feet, coming out of the position in much the same way you got into it, but landing on your feet rather than in the squat headstand.

The headstand may be done with the body piked (photo 2.4), straight or arched (photo 2.5), but the hips and legs must make different compensations in each of these three positions so that the net result keeps the center of gravity over the triangular base at all times. Once you achieve proficiency in holding the headstand you can move your legs into different positions. Try stride splits, right (photo 2.6), left (photo 2.7) and straddle splits (photo 2.8). The knees may be bent and straightened in various combinations. Lowering with straight legs so that your toes come within an inch of touching the floor, and then raising them back up again is especially valuable.

The possibilities inherent in the headstand were codified in hatha yoga over two thousand years ago. Yogis practiced inverted equilibristics long before modern competitive gymnastics was developed. Most of the symmetrical yoga asanas (postures) have been incorporated into western acrobatics, whereas the asymmetrical ones are generally less familiar. The headstand we have been discussing is known in hatha yoga as *salamba sirsansana II. Salamba sirsansana I*

PHOTO 2.4

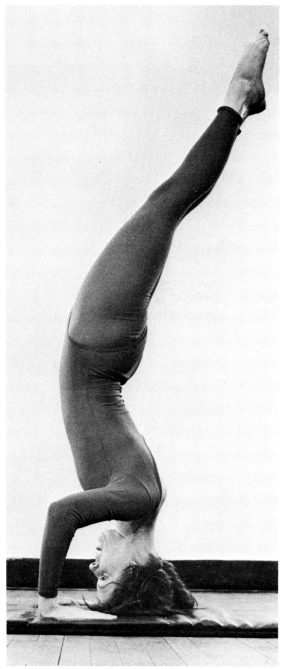

PHOTO 2.5

PHOTO 2.6

PHOTO 2.7

PHOTO 2.8

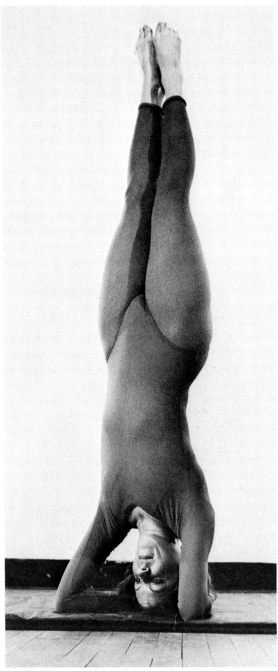

PHOTO 2.9

is a headstand frequently associated with yoga. In this variation, the elbows are placed where the hands would be and the hands are wrapped, one over the other, around the back of the head, so that the body is supported on the head and forearms (photo 2.9). This base is also triangular in shape.

Buster Keaton used a headstand for comic effect in the motion picture *The Balloonatic* (First National, 1923). He wades into a stream to do some fishing, confident that his hip boots will keep him dry. So intent is he on fishing, that he goes in too deep and the boots are quickly flooded. In order to empty them without troubling to take them off, he goes up into a headstand.

Handstand

Many people have the mistaken idea that handstands require exceptional strength. This is not the case. If kept straight, your arms will support you for at least a few seconds. You only need enough strength to hold your body in a fixed position. However, you do need help to learn a handstand. Until you know how to come down from it safely, you should not attempt it without someone there to hold you.

Some instructors advocate learning the handstand with your feet against a wall. This may give you the strength and stamina needed to practice the handstand for longer periods of time, but it will not really help you with the balance. If you lack such strength, however, this method is paradoxically dangerous. For these reasons, I do not recommend it to my students.

You may learn the handstand on the floor,

on low parallel bars, on handstand blocks or on parallelettes; the differences are not great. To do the handstand on the floor, bend one knee forward, place the hands shoulder-distance apart with the fingers curved so that the knuckles are slightly off the floor (photo 2.10a). Scissor up (kicking one leg at a time) as gently as possible so that your weight is not thrown too far forward (photo 2.10b). Keep the arms straight. Stretch through the shoulders, lift toward the ceiling with the body fairly straight, press the legs together and point the toes (photo 2.10c). Once you are comfortable with this approach, you should try kicking up with the other leg or kicking both legs up together.

If you begin to overbalance, push the fingertips into the floor. If you underbalance, push with the heels of your hands and bend the elbows slightly. Once your elbows are bent, however, it is difficult to regain a good balance. The best solution is to slightly overbalance throughout the handstand so that there is a constant, steady pressure on the fingertips.

Some students feel more comfortable arched or piked. A "correct" handstand in competitive gymnastics must be done with the body in a straight line, although at one time an arched handstand constituted "correct" form. When it comes to circus techniques, however, if you stay up it does not matter what form you are using.

When using low parallel bars, grip one bar in each hand and kick up into the handstand as before (photo 2.11a). There are two reasons for learning with the mini-parallel bars. Your wrists will not get as sore because they

PHOTO 2.10a

PHOTO 2.10b

PHOTO 2.10c

PHOTO 2.11a

PHOTO 2.11b

PHOTO 2.11c

are not required to be bent back. You will also have more leverage rocking forward and backward with your hands using the bars than without them.

Perhaps the best dismount from the over-balanced handstand, particularly on the low parallel bars, consists of twisting the hips into the second half of a cartwheel (chapter six). If you twist your hips to the right, your left hand would be lifted and placed in a cartwheel position in front of your right hand (photo 2.11b). Your eyes remain focused on a spot between your hands. You land in a squat position on both feet, bringing them in close to the hands (photo 2.11c).

When using handstand blocks, their seven-degree slope pitches the body forward, and this can help you stay up (photo 2.12). The hands grip the blocks with the fingers bent over the lowered front end and the thumbs bent over the insides. The main advantages of both the low parallel bars and the handstand blocks are combined in individual parallel bars or parallelettes (photo 2.13).

The handstand we have been discussing is known in hatha yoga as *adho mukha vrksasana*. There are many other asanas that are handstands, variations of the handstand or include phases that are handstands. For instance, *pincha mayurasana* is a forearm stand. This posture frees the hands—possibly to do plate spinning (chapter seven). *Sayanasana* is almost the same except that the hands are lifted up under the chin, leaving the body balanced on the elbows. *Muyurasana* is a bent arm handstand with the body horizontal and the fingers pointing toward the feet. *Hamasana* is the same thing,

PHOTO 2.12

but with the hands reversed so the fingers are pointing toward the head. If you are as intrigued by these variations as I am, I would refer you to *Light on Yoga* by B. K. S. Iyengar (New York: Shocken Books, 1965). Available in paperback, it gives many more variations.

Walking on the hands

Walking on the hands is somewhat analagous to balancing a cue stick (chapter one). The body stays fairly straight, while the support shifts from side to side, first on the left hand and then on the right. Some people find walking on their hands easier than maintaining a stationary handstand. Johann Huslinger found it so easy that in 1900 he walked on his hands from Vienna to Paris, covering a distance of 871 miles (l,402 kilometers) in 55 days; he averaged ten hours per day and 1.58 m.p.h. (2.54 k.p.h.).

Walking on the hands may be one of the very few circus techniques in which men generally have an advantage over women. It is not unusual for a man with broad shoulders to learn to walk on his hands before he can hold a handstand, whereas initially a woman frequently cannot support all her weight on one arm, even briefly.

To walk on your hands, do a handstand and slightly overbalance forward. Take small "steps" so that you stay a bit off balance forward (photo 2.14). Your steps must match the amount of forward lean of your body. If you step without leaning forward you will lose the balance backward, but the more the body leans forward, the bigger and/or faster the steps must be.

PHOTO 2.13

PHOTO 2.14

Once you can walk in a straight line you may want to try turning around, walking in a circle (clockwise and counterclockwise) and putting the legs in different positions as you walk. You could, for example, alternate right and left stride splits with your legs as you walk on your hands. Some people find it easier to bend their knees and/or keep their legs apart as they walk. You could also clap your feet together or carry something between them for comic effect.

Buster Keaton walked on his hands in a chase scene in the motion picture *The Scarecrow* (Metro Pictures Corporation, 1920). Wanting to get to the other side of a shallow river without getting his feet wet, he decides to walk across on his hands. He dives into the water, landing on his hands in a handstand, and successfully walks across with his feet dry. Once he has practically reached the other bank, he goes into a backbend (chapter six) in order to plant his feet on solid ground. At the last moment, however, he loses his balance and collapses into the stream, totally soaking himself.

Basic principles

Carlo Mazzone-Clementi calls the headstand a "brainwash" because it brings more blood to the head and improves circulation. In terms of circus techniques, overcoming the confusion of balancing upside-down on the ground should give you valuable insights into being upside-down on the trapeze (chapter eight), or while tumbling (chapter six), and will even help you to balance while right side up (chapter five). All of these positions lend themselves to proper breathing and relaxation, and are therefore an excellent preparation for the more advanced circus skills.

In India, the birthplace of yoga, the rejuvenating effects of hatha yoga asanas are pursued as an end unto themselves and so that the practitioner will live long enough to complete the difficult journey to enlightenment. Likewise, members of the Cheyenne Indian contrary societies found another way these techniques could prolong one's life span. The contraries played the clown in everyday life, doing everything contrary to the norm (backward, upside-down, etc.). They were particularly noted for their ability to walk on their hands and to walk, run or ride backwards. In battle they reverted to normal postures and, because their "circus" training had given them new strength and awareness, they turned out to be the fiercest warriors of all and were seldom killed in combat.

Free headstand

A free headstand is an inverted balance on just the head with no support from the hands. This is what circus performers are usually referring to when they speak of a headstand. It is usually done with the aid of a grommet (a round, padded support which fits the top of the head). Before learning the free headstand, you should be able to balance in a regular headstand with your back straight and your legs apart and horizontal. As a preparation, shift your weight so it is more over your head and then maintain your balance as you slowly lift up the hands until only the thumbs are in contact with the floor.

Another preparatory exercise would be to see how many times you can consecutively clap your hands together without losing your balance. Then try taking your hands away and maintaining the balance by bending and straightening alternate legs. It may be easier to learn this on an elevated support, such as a stool, so that the shoulders can be dropped and the arms can be below the support. This creates less tension and lowers the center of gravity, therefore making it easier to balance. Eventually you may be able to balance with the legs together and straight up.

One-arm handstand

A one-arm handstand on the floor is difficult. It is easier to learn on pommels (handstand blocks mounted on flexible steel rods fixed to a base). You must first be able to do a straight two-arm handstand with the body stretched up as far as possible. When beginning the one-arm handstand the legs are apart and can be either straight or bent at the knees. You cannot simply lift up one arm, but instead must slowly transfer your weight so that eventually one arm supports all the weight. Extend the supporting shoulder, squeeze the block tightly and balance with the other hand barely touching its block. Ideally this would also be learned with the other arm.

A more direct method of getting into the one-arm handstand is used by women in the Shenyang Acrobatic Troupe. They put one arm on the support, slowly bring the back leg up beyond a split and, without the aid of the other hand, shift their weight completely to the supporting arm.

Leonid Yengibarov performed the best comic handbalancing act that I have ever seen. With the ring bathed in red light, he began his entrée by executing a two-arm handstand that was perfect in every respect except that one foot was flexed. Finally the pointed foot slowly flexed and pointed again, hooking under the flexed foot and pushing it up into the "correct" (i.e. pointed) position. He then very, very slowly lowered his body down to a horizontal position, supported only by his hands. He then took one hand off the floor, leaving himself in what is called a one-arm lever, with his legs crossed and with his eyes shaded by his free hand à la Buster Keaton (photo 2.15). This position was also held for an unusual length of time. Finally, he lowered himself down to the floor and fell a-sleep. The whole routine was so unbelievably slow and so incredible to watch that it brought the house down.

Marinelli bend

The Marinelli bend is a balance on a mouthpiece with the body in a close backbend. It requires a backbend good enough to allow you to rest your rear end on your head. A student I observed at the Moscow Circus School worked on it by doing a backbend over the bar holding the mouthpiece. After biting the mouthpiece, the next step was to take her feet off the floor and the final step was to lift her hands off the floor. This is all done very, very slowly, and the mouthpiece must be specially designed for the performer's own mouth and teeth.

PHOTO 2.15

3

In vertical vaulting, the performer simply jumps upward, downward, forward, backward or sideways without any external assistance and without substantial rotation of the body. The jumps may be of a particular height and distance and may also be made over, between, under or through animate or inanimate obstacles. The rotation of the body will be added in chapter six (tumble vaulting) and the use of external assistance in chapter nine (catapult vaulting). Once again, no special equipment is required.

As in the first two chapters, the performer might be a marine mammal, in this case the bottle-nose dolphin (*Tursiops trucatus*), some of whose spectacular leaps in the air have drawn audiences from all over the world to their performances in Florida and California. Australia's red kangaroo (*Macropus rufus*) and great gray kangaroo (*Macropus canguru*) have been known to make leaps exceeding forty feet (12.2 meters). The human flea (*Pulex irritans*) is able to jump about two hundred times its body length. Of course the universal importance of jumping in sports, games, pastimes and dance hardly needs to be demonstrated.

Jumping, circus and physical fitness

Most of my classes begin with the whole class being led in a series of warm-up and conditioning exercises. These include various ways of walking, running, skipping, galloping, hopping and, above all, jumping: little jumps, big jumps, broad jumps, trying to touch the ceiling and so forth. These are

Vertical vaulting

done by the entire class simultaneously or in rapid succession.

These warm-up exercises emphasize flexibility, strength, equilibrium, coordination and endurance (aerobics), all factors which make for well-rounded physical conditioning. The need for physical fitness is generally recognized, but approaches to the subject tend to run in cycles, emphasizing isolated aspects. Isometrics concentrated on strength, demonstrating that it was resistance itself and not heavy weights that was needed to build up muscles. When it was discovered that strength could not be equated with total fitness, pliometrics became popular as a means of developing greater flexibility. The most current fashion is aerobics, which concentrates on creating greater cardiovascular capacity and therefore greater endurance. I see nothing inherently wrong with any of these methods, but I do believe that a carefully selected program of "exercise" drawn from circus techniques can be the ultimate physical conditioning. These techniques are based on flexibility, strength, equilibrium, coordination and endurance, and they develop these attributes to their highest potential.

Rope jumping and skipping

Skipping and jumping rope is an excellent activity that combines the three fundamental circus elements: jugglery, equilibrium and jumping. As a popular pastime, jumping rope can be traced at least as far back as ancient Egypt, where the hieroglyph of a stick figure jumping rope is the character for the determinative "to skip." Although nowadays it is sometimes dismissed as effeminate, jumping rope was exclusively a boy's activity until the early part of this century. In my own classes, I usually find there are a few male students who have never jumped rope. Today, males usually do it only as a means of training for sports such as boxing, and not as a game in itself. It is not coincidental that Muhammad Ali, who probably has the fastest footwork of any heavyweight boxer in history, is also phenomenal at jumping rope. In recent years, rope jumping has become more popular and taken on more importance as a part of aerobics because it builds up more endurance than do equal periods of rowing, volleyball, jogging or cycling.

We usually begin by "skipping" rope. Instead of keeping the feet together, you put one foot through and then the other (photos 3.1a-c). This is much easier, because if you get the first foot through, you have it made. The rope does not have to billow out so much because it is passing under a narrower (one foot) obstacle. Once you feel comfortable "skipping" rope, you should also be able to "jump" rope. The two feet go through together (photos 3.2a-b). You may find it helpful to make an additional jump while the rope is passing over your head. You should definitely try both of these methods in a forward and in a backward direction.

Jumping rope requires little or no instruction. People automatically improve if they simply keep practicing it because they generally do not develop bad habits that would impede their progress. However, if there are any initial difficulties, they may be due to one of the following mistakes.

Problems may arise if you try to pull your knees up as high as possible. This is not necessarily wrong, and it is more beneficial in terms of aerobics, but it is not the most efficient method, particularly for a beginner. Too much focus is then put on jumping high and not enough attention is given to what the rope itself is doing. The rope is less than half an inch (1.27 cm) thick, and that is as far as your feet have to get off the ground in order to clear it. A good boxer does it with his feet barely off the floor.

Lack of balance can also cause difficulties. The spine should be kept reasonably vertical. Some people throw their shoulders back and forth, lose their balance as a result, and then waste a lot of energy trying to regain it. Others swing their arms too much. The rope handles can stay almost at a fixed point if the rope is the proper length (stretching from armpit to armpit under the feet). Some people hit the back of their necks because they are going down with their hands when the rope is going up, and going up with their hands when the rope is going down. If you want to make any up and down movement with the arms, they should go down when the rope is going down, and up when the rope is going up.

Once the basic technique has been mastered, you might try to pass the rope under your feet twice during one jump. As many as five turns of the rope have been done on a single jump. Other variations can be added, and the permutations are almost limitless:

PHOTO 3.1a

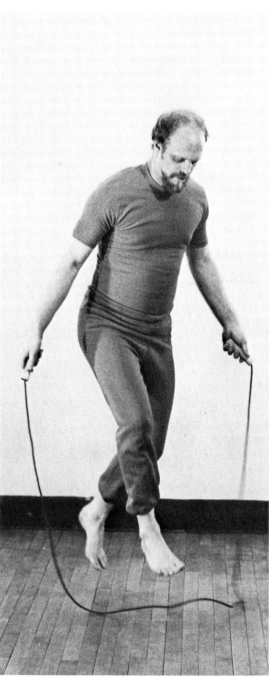

PHOTO 3.1b

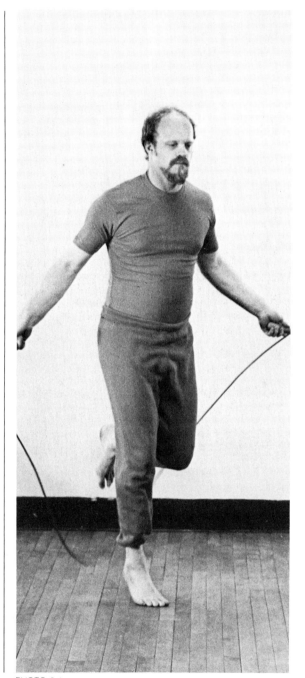

PHOTO 3.1c

26 Circus techniques

PHOTO 3.2a

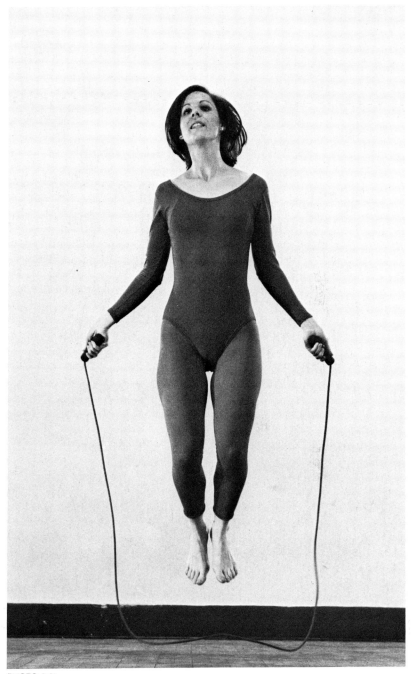

PHOTO 3.2b

Vertical vaulting 27

hopping on just one foot: holding both ends of the rope in one hand; jumping to the side (it is hard to get the back hand in an effective position); crossing the rope in front of you so that the left and right hands switch places (photo 3.3); and even jumping rope while lying on one's back. For other possibilities, the reader is referred to *Jump Rope!* by Peter L. Skolnik (New York: Workman Publishing Co., 1974) and Roy Ald's *Jump for Joy* (New York: Bernard Geis Associates, 1971).

Of course rope can also be jumped with two other people holding the ends of the rope. In this way, two ropes can be used and two or more people can jump at the same time. You can also tie one end of the rope to a secure point and swing the other end with your arm as you jump over the rope. This is precisely what Buster Keaton does in *My Wife's Relations* (First National, 1922). He is kneading a large piece of saltwater taffy on a spike. He pounds and stretches it, and during one stretch the taffy sags dangerously in the middle. Keaton suddenly starts "jumping taffy," swinging the loose end with his hand.

Hoop Jumping

A large hoop, such as a hula hoop about 36 inches (91.44 cm) in diameter, can be used in much the same way as a jump rope. Hold the hoop in front of you, framing your face with the bottom of the hoop at about your navel. Hold it at the bottom, knuckles up with the hands about a foot (30.48 cm) apart (photo 3.4a). Begin to rotate the top of the hoop forward and downward (photo 3.4b) and jump over and through it before it reaches

PHOTO 3.3

PHOTO 3.4a

PHOTO 3.4b

PHOTO 3.4c

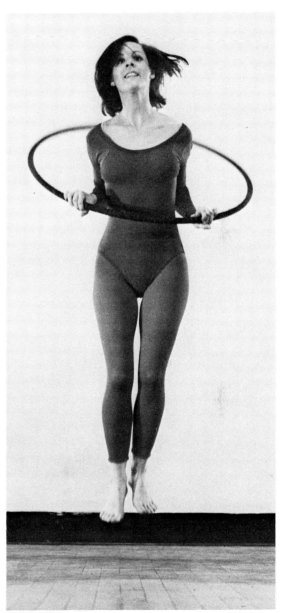

PHOTO 3.4d

your ankles (photo 3.4c). Continue to rotate it behind your back (photo 3.4d) up over your head to the starting position. It may also be necessary to lower the whole hoop slightly when it is in the down position in order to clear it on your jump. If you need to do this. do not neglect to raise it about the same amount above the norm by the time it is in the up position in order to avoid hitting yourself on the back of the head. You cannot see this. but if you neglect to do it you will certainly feel it. To make repeated jumps in rhythm you can use gravity. centrifugal force and inertia of motion to keep the hoop rotating. Loosen your grip on the hoop by simply pressing the tip of your index fingers to the end of your thumbs so that the hoop can turn freely. Once started. a slightly circular up-and-down movement of the hands can keep the hoop rotating around you as you jump. To jump backwards. reverse the rotation. Start in the same position. but rotate the hoop backward over your head. down behind you and forward toward your feet and ankles as you jump over and bring the hoop to the initial position.

Stick jumping

It is advisable to jump through a prepared wire coat hanger before attempting to jump over a stick. To prepare the coat hanger. unwind the wire at the top. open the sides to right angles and use athletic training tape to fasten the excess wire to the sides and cover any sharp points. Gently gripping the coat hanger in your fingertips. hold it straight up over your head and bend your knees in prep-aration to jump (photo 3.5a). Swing the coat hanger down as you jump (photo 3.5b) and back under your feet as you reach the peak of your jump (photo 3.5c). Land on your feet in a plié with the coat hanger behind you (photo 3.5d).

Most people are surprised that they can do this. Some people jump over the coat hanger through sheer speed: They quickly jump up. swing the coat hanger under. and get back down again. They are swinging the coat hanger as *slowly* as possible and jumping through the opening as fast as they can. Others do it through flexibility: Their timing may be way off. but they are able to pull their knees up much higher than they need to. You will find it harder to do it backwards because you cannot get as good a windup with the arms.

After you have jumped over the coat hanger in both directions, you may begin to gradually choke up on the coat hanger, eliminating—a little at a time—the extra eight inches (20.32 cm) of leeway that it provides. In this way you can progress to the point where you will have the confidence to jump over a flexible stick (photo 3.6), a doubled-up jump rope (photo 3.7), a cane (photo 3.8), or even a stilt (photo 3.9).

Basic principles

Jumping is movement through space. what Georges Hébert. the French movement specialist, has labeled "impulsive motility." This is the opposite of "articulate motility." which is movement without going anywhere, the most extreme example of which would be

PHOTO 3.5a

PHOTO 3.5b

PHOTO 3.5c

PHOTO 3.5d

PHOTO 3.6

PHOTO 3.7

PHOTO 3.8

PHOTO 3.9

contortion. When you do move through space, you must push against something in order to propel yourself forward. In jumping, the body must rely on its own kinetic energy to overcome the downward pull of gravity. This kinetic energy will depend on the mass of the body and its speed, so that the height of a jump is determined by the speed at which the body leaves the ground.

The push-off from the ground operates on Newtonian principles: For every action there is an equal and opposite reaction. As far back as ancient Greece, jumpers threw stone weights behind them as they jumped so as to increase the opposite reaction that was their jump. This is also why it is difficult to take off from sand: The sand gives way, reducing the thrust of the push-off action. On the other hand, it is easier to land in sand, sawdust or on a mat, because the force of the jump will be partially absorbed.

Once the body has left the ground, it is governed by the laws of falling objects, which—as Galileo demonstrated—are the same for heavy and light objects. This is why a flea must have the same take-off speed as a man in order to jump one foot (30.48 cm) up off the ground. The smaller the mass, however, the less thrust the legs will have to provide in order to achieve a given take-off speed.

Once in the air, an acrobat can twist and turn at different speeds in order to land on his feet but, because he is also a falling object, he cannot alter his trajectory. This is why catapult vaulting (chapter nine) is so dangerous: If, for example, you hit the bed of a trampoline at an angle that catapults your body off the trampoline, there is little you can do about it. You cannot pull your weight back on to the trampoline once you are no longer over it.

High jump and broad jump

It just so happens that jumping is something that can be measured, so obviously you can go for extremes of height and/or distance. As a result of competition, achievement in jumping forward and upward has been developed to a high degree, but unfortunately this has been to the neglect of jumping sideways and backward. The channeling of jumping into competitive events has become overly structured and un-improvisational. In some respects, however, the jumping done in track and field borders on the kind of athleticism we also find in circus. The competition is not merely one jumper against another, but one jumper competing against his previous marks. It is more like trying to turn a record-breaking number of somersaults on the flying trapeze. You are trying to clear this obstacle or that distance, and the relevance of competitors is not so great.

In *College* (Metro Picture Corporation, 1927), Buster Keaton tries to make the grade as a track and field star. On his first try at the high jump, he knocks the bar off with his chest and gets it tangled between his legs. On his second attempt, he breaks the bar in two with his chest. He tries to put the bar back up, having thrown half of it away, but it is too short. He gets a new bar and does several successful but very low jumps. He then raises it up to the highest position, measures his distance three or four times, does a funny run and—the bar falls off just as he gets to it. Finally he does a tiger leap (chapter six) over the bar head first into the sawdust, where he remains kicking until someone comes along and pulls him out.

Part two

Pure forms

In toss juggling, the performer keeps several inanimate objects in the air at the same time by alternately tossing and catching them. One is said to be juggling if the number of objects is larger than the number of points of contact that are being used to throw and catch them. Therefore, you would have to do at least two objects in one hand or three objects in two hands to be juggling in this sense.

Historically, toss juggling dates back at least as far as ancient Egypt. The earliest evidence we have comes from the tombs of Beni Hassan (1900 B.C.), in which several women are depicted juggling balls (photo 4.1). Toss juggling is a rather abstract activity and its fascination seems to be limited to human beings. Enrico Rastelli, one of the best and most famous jugglers of all time, regarded juggling as a form of consciousness expansion and maintained that it was one of the most worthwhile of human endeavors. For many people, it can become a transcendental activity, much like meditation with attendant revelations and so forth.

The subject matter of this chapter is unique in that I have never seen any animal, other than the human being (*Homo sapiens*), function in this area. I have seen the California sea lion balance a ball on its nose (chapter one) and the European brown bear (*Ursus arctos*) perform a back somersault through the air from a teeterboard (chapter nine), but I have never seen an animal toss juggle. Several trainers have taught the European brown bear to foot juggle with a cylinder, even one flaming at both ends, but this is gyroscopic juggling (chapter seven), and therefore not at all the same thing.

4

Toss juggling

PHOTO 4.1

Two balls in one hand

In chapter one, we began by trying to balance a cue stick on the palm of the hand. This simple activity can give you an insight into toss juggling. In my classes, I mount a wooden ball with a hole drilled in it on a slender stick. I balance the stick and ball on the palm of my hand (photo 4.2a) and then let the stick slide between my fingers (photo 4.2b). Invariably the stick will fall on the floor and the ball into my hand (photo 4.2c). That is precisely the relationship between balance juggling and toss juggling.

We could even take this one step further and spindle two balls on a stick like shishkebab (photo 4.3). This would not quite work because the the two balls would not be able to pass each other, but it is an approximation of what we are going to do. In order to juggle two balls in one hand, we will have to throw them in such a way that they do not collide. A common tendency is to throw the second ball in front of the first one, so that each succeeding throw is further in front of you. With each throw your chances of catching them are bound to be considerably reduced. The best method is to keep your throws in a flat plane in front of you. Each throw is sent a bit to the outside, just enough to clear the other ball. The trajectory is parabolic and goes from the inside to the outside. Your hand catches each ball near the side of your hips and then moves somewhat toward the center of your body in order to make the throw.

PHOTO 4.2a

PHOTO 4.2b

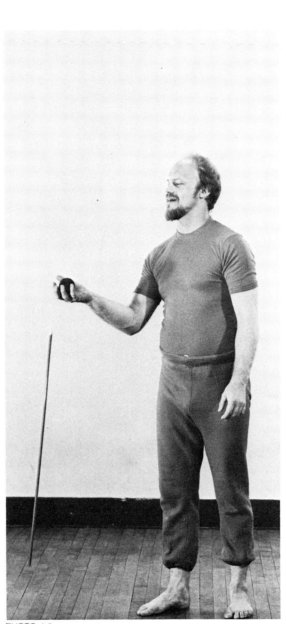

PHOTO 4.2c

PHOTO 4.3

The timing of the throws is such that the balls stay diametrically opposed. It is analagous to using two buckets at opposite ends of a rope to draw water from a well. When you are pulling the water up in one bucket, you are automatically lowering the other bucket for the next load of water. There is also this same kind of doubling up of activity in juggling, except it is continuous and more circular.

So the first exercise is to juggle two balls in one hand (photo 4.4a). Try to throw one ball up and to the outside (photo 4.4b), and when this ball reaches the highest point of its arc (photo 4.4c), throw the second ball along the same trajectory (photo 4.4d). When the second ball reaches the highest point of its arc, the first ball is being caught (photo 4.4e). Hold the first ball with your ring finger and pinky as the second ball descends (photo 4.4f). Without reaching up for it, catch the second ball with your thumb, index finger and middle finger (photo 4.4g).

The ball slows down as it goes up and speeds up as it comes down, but the amount of time it takes to go from the lowest point to the highest point is equal to the time it takes to go from the highest point to the lowest point. Therefore, if you throw each ball at the correct time, it is quite easy to keep them diametrically opposed.

The nearer the ball to your hand, the faster its speed, whether it is rising or falling. The further the ball from your hand, the slower it is traveling, whether it is moving up or down. You must be able to grasp this neutral moment in order to juggle two balls in one hand, three balls in two hands, or four balls in two

PHOTO 4.4a

PHOTO 4.4b

PHOTO 4.4c

PHOTO 4.4d

PHOTO 4.4e

PHOTO 4.4f

PHOTO 4.4g

hands. This built-in signal that it is time to make the next throw does not apply to five, six or seven balls.

Optimum throws range anywhere from about eye level to about one foot (30.48 cm) above your head (photos 4.4c and 4.4e). Once you choose a height, every ball should be thrown to this height. It will probably be easier to hold the two balls in a line parallel to the axis of your forearm rather than a line intersecting the forearm axis (photo 4.4a). You hold the front ball—which will be thrown first—with the index finger, middle finger and thumb, while the second ball is held against the heel of the hand with the pinky and ring finger. The second ball can be thrown either from its original position or it can first be rolled down the hand to the same position the first ball occupied. The throw is basically a flick of the wrist. Be careful that the hand does not follow through. It should not move upward with the ball.

In all the juggling you do, it will be important to keep your arms in the correct position (photos 4.4a-g). Although we can safely assume that the forearm should be parallel to the floor, this does not mean that you simply bend your arm at the elbow to form a 90° angle with the upper arm which would then be perpendicular to the floor. This will only produce tension in your shoulder, and this will interfere with your juggling. The best position places your elbow back so that it can counterbalance the weight of your hand and the juggling balls. You should have just enough tension in the elbow to maintain the position, but your shoulder should be completely relaxed. The hands should remain at this level for catching each throw. Let the ball

fall into your hand rather than reaching up to grab it.

You look at each ball at the top of its arc (photos 4.4c and 4.4e), and *not* at your hands, just as you would focus on the top of the cue stick in order to balance it on the palm of your hand. This tells you two things. First of all, when the ball reaches the peak of its arc, you know it is time to make your next throw. It also tells you where to move your hand to catch that ball if your throw was anything less than perfect.

Once you succeed in doing at least a "flash" (each ball goes up and down once) of two balls in one hand, you should then try to do the same in your opposite hand. When you can flash two balls in either hand, you are ready to work on three balls in two hands.

Three-ball cascade

The pattern for the three-ball cascade is very similar to braiding hair. If you are right-handed, you will probably want to start with two balls in your right hand and one in the left. The first ball in your right hand is thrown to a point opposite your left shoulder and above your left hand. When this first ball reaches the peak of its arc, the ball in the left hand is thrown under the first ball to a parallel point opposite your right shoulder (photo 4.5). As this second ball peaks, the ball still remaining in your right hand is thrown exactly the same as the first throw. If you can catch all three balls in the opposite hand, so that you end up with two balls in your left hand and one in the right, you have successfully completed a flash of three balls. Mastering this crisscross pattern is your first objective in three-ball juggling.

PHOTO 4.5

Although it may be far more poetic to think of it as triangular, the path of the throws is actually parabolic. In fact, Aristotle taught that bodies cannot have two motions at once and therefore a projectile was believed to move in two straight lines. A pre-Newtonian treatise on how to shoot cannonballs explains that they are shot to a point directly above the target and then drop vertically onto it. It was Galileo who finally discovered that a projectile moves in a curved path (a parabola) and not in two straight lines. However, armies had made successful use of cannons long before Galileo and Newton and, although the Egyptians apparently had nothing approaching Newtonian mathematics, they still knew how to juggle. The person who can figure something out with a slide rule cannot necessarily do it. We are interested in doing it.

The most important thing I can tell someone who is trying to flash three balls is to make sure that they get all their throws to the same height and at the same angle. Your throws, as seen in profile, must be vertical, and if you insist on throwing one or more balls way out in front of you, your progress will be considerably slower. There is a certain point beyond which even a good juggler cannot handle inaccurate throws.

Another common mistake is to try to juggle too fast when progressing from two in one hand to three in two hands. Actually, three balls is a slower tempo because you have fewer balls per hand.

Some people tend to make their three-ball pattern too narrow because they have grown accustomed to doing two balls in one hand. It is best to keep your hands about shoulder-width apart. If the height of your throws is about shoulder level then you will be tossing each ball at approximately a 45° angle.

If you throw and catch each ball once, you have completed a flash of three balls. With this flash, you know what the cascade pattern is, you know what ball juggling is and you know what toss juggling is. However, in order to make a continuum out of it, you have to go beyond a flash. This means making a fourth throw, and a fifth throw, and so on, continuing to juggle in the same pattern. This continuum can go on to infinity, for you never have more than one ball in either hand at a given moment.

If you are having difficulty going further, you should try to complete a flash starting with two balls in the opposite hand. This is tantamount to the fourth throw, for if you can flash starting with two in the right or two in the left, you already have a sense of that continuity. I have found that it helps to count your throws up to about the tenth one, after which the differentiation becomes less clear. When you are just learning, you might find that you consistently miss the seventh throw and need to concentrate on it, but I do not think that the same thing happens as much once you get past about ten throws. It then becomes much more of a continuum.

Three-ring cascade

There is no need to perfect three balls before you go on to three rings. In fact, one out of every three or four of my students finds rings easier to juggle than balls. There are several possible explanations for this. Some people have a smaller degree of supination in their hands than do others. This means that it is uncomfortable for them to keep their palms straight up. When you are catching and throwing rings, your palms are pretty much facing each other so that the hands do not have to supinate. Therefore, three rings are automatically easier for those people with a narrower range of supination.

The higher you throw, the slower the tempo will be. Since most rings are at least one foot (30.48 cm) in diameter, people usually realize that they must always be thrown at least this high just to avoid colliding. This is not always the case with balls, which some beginners will throw less than one foot (30.48 cm) high. Furthermore, since rings are thinner than most balls, there is less chance of their colliding.

Yet another advantage of rings stems from the fact that many beginners have a tendency to catch balls too high, near their shoulders rather than at the hips. This works fine with rings because they should be caught at shoulder level, and if they are caught in an even higher position, this is at least less wrong with rings than it would be with balls.

On the other hand, rings can also present difficulties that you did not encounter with balls. Because of the aerodynamics of rings, it is easy not to have any sense of them moving through the air. This usually results in throwing them too far forward or back over your shoulder. You are rotating your wrist on the throw, and therefore the ring must be released at the precise moment when inertia will take it in a tangent perpendicular to the floor. Another problem is that people with more fleshy webbing, or more sensitive webbing, between their thumb and forefinger often experience some pain when juggling rings. This is no doubt why very few bats juggle rings.

You should be able to flash two rings in either hand before working with three in two hands. You can hold two rings in one hand either by placing a finger between the two rings or by fanning them as if they were playing cards. For two in one hand, the rings should be tipped to the outside before they are thrown in order to get them into that same inside-outside pattern that we used to juggle two balls in one hand (photo 4.6). The angle at which the ring is held at the moment of release predetermines the angle of its trajectory; with balls the angle of the trajectory is determined by the position of the hand.

Three rings are juggled in the same cascade pattern you used to do three balls (photo 4.7). They are made to crisscross by tipping them toward the center and are caught at shoulder level with the hand grasping the bottom of the ring at the ring's "six o'clock" position. When the ring falls into your hand, it will balance momentarily between your thumb and forefinger, giving you a little extra time to close your hand.

Three sticks

We will not follow the same methodology with sticks that we did with balls and rings, because to do two sticks in one hand usually requires a double rotation of each stick, and we do not want to make things unnecessarily difficult. Assuming that you can juggle three balls, you should start by replacing the second ball you throw (the lone ball in your left hand) with a stick. The first throw is with a ball, the second with the stick, and the third

PHOTO 4 6

PHOTO 4 7

with the other ball (photo 4.8). The stick makes one complete rotation around its center of gravity, which means that you throw it from the handle and then catch the handle the next time it comes around. If you do a flash, the stick will land in the other hand.

It is important to learn this by starting with the stick in either hand. When you can keep two balls and a stick going you can then go right on to three sticks. It would be unnecessarily complicated to try to do two sticks and one ball at this point.

The pattern for three sticks is the same cascade pattern used to juggle three balls and three rings (photo 4.9). The major difference is that each throw involves a precise spin of the stick. Therefore, when you throw a stick, you have two separate things to think about: giving it the proper height and giving it the proper spin. Height is imparted by the arm and spin by the wrist. The spin will not automatically be proportional to the height.

If I take a stick and throw it with my wrist it could easily spin many times without going very high in the air. If I throw a stick without any wrist movement and slide my hand along it as I throw it so that the upward push is even on the under surface, the stick might go very high with no spin at all. There is no direct relationship between height and spin.

It may take more practice for you to learn to cascade three sticks because of the difficulties caused by the spin. In order to successfully catch each stick, you must not underturn or overturn any of your throws. It would be a good idea, however, to study the nature of the rotation when you *do* underturn or overturn a throw. Once you gain control over a single spin, you can start working on

PHOTO 4.8

PHOTO 4.9

throwing sticks with a double rotation or without any spin at all.

If you give a stick additional height and a double turn, you will have more time between throws and therefore more time to do variations. You might try to gain this extra time by throwing a stick high with just a single turn, but this takes more control. Furthermore, a high double spin actually comes into your hand more like a low single than a high single would. To learn this, you might just make one throw with a double rotation, and then drop right back into all singles. Eventually you should work toward doing a double with every throw.

Once you can cascade three sticks, you should work on gaining greater control over them. A good stick throw hardly goes up at all, but instead travels almost straight across to the other hand. I learned to cascade three sticks by making high narrow throws, and from there I worked on lowering the pattern. As they get lower and lower, the juggling gets faster and faster unless the sticks are thrown wider. If the hands are kept at shoulder-width distance, it starts getting slower again because you gain time from the width. The lower, wider pattern will result in greater control, which will make it easier to perform other variations, particularly club juggling and passing.

Juggling a ball, ring and stick

Once you feel fairly comfortable with all three types of objects, you might try mixing them by juggling one ball, one ring and one stick (photo 4.10). This is very good practice because you get to work with three basic types of objects at the same time.

When you do mix objects, your throws have to match the height of each other object's center of gravity; for a stick, this is the point around which it spins. If you can control a ball, a ring and a stick, you should be able to throw the ball through the ring while juggling. This will be easier to accomplish if the trajectories of the ring and ball are at right angles to each other. It is also possible, but more difficult, to throw the stick through the ring.

Four-ball fountain

Once you have learned to juggle three objects, you should learn to flash four balls. For the time being, you need not master four balls, but to at least have flashed them will be of tremendous help if you want to do variations with three objects. Once the fourth ball is removed, you will naturally feel that you have extra time.

The basic technique for juggling four balls has actually already been covered in our discussion of two balls in one hand. Once you have learned to do two balls in the right hand for at least a flash and two balls in the left hand for at least a flash, all that remains is to do both hands at the same time. This pattern is known as the fountain. It can be done with both hands throwing simultaneously (photo 4.11), or in opposition (right-left-right-left, etc.). It is usually better to first try it simultaneously as this will enable you to see if the balls are being thrown to the same height and in an even rhythm.

Basic principles

The exercises we have covered so far can provide a framework for all toss juggling. We

PHOTO 4.10

PHOTO 4.11

have already covered the two basic juggling patterns and the three types of objects. From these we can derive certain principles that will apply to most advanced toss juggling.

For the purposes of juggling, we divide objects into three types: *nuclear, curvilinear* and *linear.* Balls are the most common example of a nuclear object. I conceive of it as a point or nucleus with a surface that is equidistant from that point. Many objects can be considered to be nuclear and can therefore be juggled just like balls: apples (photo 4.12), alarm clocks, bunches of grapes, etc.—in fact, just about anything you can get your hand under or around. Even an object as big as a basketball can be juggled in this manner if you can get your hand under its center of gravity and push the object up.

The next category is curvilinear objects, such as rings or plates (photo 4.13). Other common examples include hoops, frisbees and hats. It would be going too far to say that someone who has developed an act with rings or plates could switch to the other right away. In general, plates are more difficult than rings, but not to someone who has been working with them consistently. I find that for odd numbers a ring is much easier to grasp than a plate because you can close your hand around its rim as if it were a stick, whereas plates can give you a cramp in the hand if you are not used to them.

The final category is linear objects. Examples include sticks, clubs (photo 4.14), torches, knives, hammers and tennis rackets. They should be weighted at one end so as to put the turning point further away from the handle. As with sticks, they are usually juggled with one full rotation per throw.

PHOTO 4.12

PHOTO 4.13

PHOTO 4.14

These same three categories appear in the reminiscences of a nineteenth-century British juggler, as recorded by Henry Mayhew:

Juggling is the same now as ever it was, for there ain't been no improvement on the old style as I ever heard on; an suppose that balls and knives and rings will last a hundred years to come yet.*

At this point, you should have an understanding of the fundamentals of toss juggling. This framework should give you a sound basis for continued work with your juggling. More detailed instruction is found in the next section, but the reader is encouraged to invent and reinvent, discover and rediscover his own variations as much as possible.

Numbers juggling

Adding more objects is referred to as *numbers juggling,* and particularly applies to four or more objects. It is not necessarily the essence of juggling.

The work you have already done prepares you for juggling larger numbers of objects. The cascade pattern used to juggle three balls will be used to juggle any odd number of objects (5, 7, 9, 11, 13, etc.). The fountain pattern used to juggle four balls can be used to juggle any even number of objects. To do four balls, we juggled two balls in each hand. To juggle six balls, you would have to be able to juggle three balls in each hand at the same time; eight balls would be four in each hand, and so forth.

Enrico Rastelli (1896-1931) could apparently juggle ten balls, but the most I have ever seen successfully juggled in the air is

seven, and I have only seen two people do that: Sergei Ignatov of the Soviet Union and Rudy Horn of Germany. Unless you know juggling well, any number over five is almost impossible to count in the air. You have to count them in the hands before they are thrown, and the layman never seems to bother to do that.

Many of the greatest jugglers have been able to juggle more rings than balls. This is at least partly because rings are thinner than balls. There is less chance of a collision and you can hold more of them in your hand—or easily remove them from a holster (as Ignatov does) or from your mouth (as Albert Petrovsky does). They also tend to stay on course better because they are slightly gyroscopic. Petrovsky of the Moscow Circus did eleven rings in performance for a while, and Ignatov does eleven in practice while he performs nine. However, if we are to believe the historian Xenophon, the record still belongs to a woman juggler in Ancient Greece:

At that, the other girl began to accompany the dancer on the flute, and a boy at her elbow handed her up the hoops until he had given her twelve. She took these and as she danced kept throwing them whirling into the air, observing the proper height to throw them so as to catch them in a regular rhythm. As Socrates looked on he remarked: "This girl's feat, gentlemen, is only one of many proofs that woman's nature is really not a whit inferior to man's, except in its lack of judgment and physical strength."*

It is far more difficult to juggle a large number of linear objects. Five clubs is considered to be quite an accomplishment. Alex-

ander Kiss mastered six sticks using triple turns. Rastelli used double turns to juggle six sticks. The world's record for linear objects, however, probably belongs to Mitica Virjoaga of Rumania, who has juggled seven clubs in practice.

You will recall that the basic pattern we used for four balls was to juggle two balls in each hand in an inside-to-outside pattern called the fountain. In the reverse fountain, each ball travels from the outside to the inside. The right and left hand can throw at the same time or in opposition. Once you are comfortable doing the fountain with simultaneous throws and with alternating left and right throws. you can try changing the pattern back and forth between these two rhythms. Four objects can also be juggled in vertical lanes. Each object goes straight up and down in counterpoint to the other object being thrown by the same hand. When doing four clubs, Europeans usually fountain them, whereas Americans tend to put them in lanes (photo 4.15).

As we have already seen, any odd number of objects is most easily juggled in the same cascade pattern used for three objects. This of course applies to five balls. You will begin with three balls in your right hand and two in your left. You then throw right-left-right-left-right in a high cascade. Once you can catch all five balls, you have done a flash and laid the foundation for making a continuum out of it. By far the hardest thing about juggling five objects is that there is no demarcation as to when the next object should be thrown. You do not throw the next ball when a given ball is at the top of its arc above that hand, but slightly before that moment.

*Henry Mayhew, *London Labour and the London Poor,* Vol. III (London: Griffin, Bohn, 1861)

*Xenophon, *The Banquet,* trans. by O. J. Todd (Cambridge: Harvard University Press, 1922).

Five clubs is far more difficult than five balls or five rings. Although it is possible to do it with triples, it is usually done with double spins (photo 4.16). The key to keeping five objects going is to make those throws very, very precise. When I was learning five clubs, I thought that it was natural for the throws to be sloppy—after all, I was doing five clubs. However, when I saw Ignatov juggle five clubs, I realized that it is imperative for every club to be thrown to exactly the same height and at exactly the same angle. There is simply less margin for error with five clubs than with three.

While numbers juggling need not be your ultimate goal, it can be tremendously valuable to work on one more object than you think you can handle. This is why I start my students on four balls very early. I know the experience will make it easier for them to work on variations with three balls. Likewise, I feel that when Ignatov performs variations with five rings, this work is based on his ability to do seven, or even eleven, rings. In the Moscow Circus School, the juggling students soon find themselves working on four and five clubs rather than on all the variations possible with three. After they can do four or five, any three-club routine will have the potential for being just that much better.

Pattern variations

It is possible to disrupt the rhythm of the basic three-ball cascade with any series of moves, spins, balances or breaks that change the pattern into something else. Ideally these transitions should be crisp and come as a surprise to the audience. For

PHOTO 4.15

PHOTO 4.16

example, in the movie *The Old Fashioned Way* (Paramount, 1934), W. C. Fields is juggling four balls for a theatre audience. Suddenly, as if he had no control over it, one ball pops out of his hand and is caught by an assistant, as Fields drops into a three-ball cascade. The assistant then throws the ball back towards him and Fields takes it back into a four-ball fountain. He is seemingly oblivious to this complicated, technical feat—throwing it away—to create a wonderful comic moment.

The permutations with three objects are limitless. There is a feeling among some jugglers that you are only as good as what you can do with three objects. They are not interested in the quantity of objects you can juggle, but only in the number of variations you can perform with three.

Perhaps no variation is more basic than the reverse cascade. Instead of throwing each object under the previous throw, it is thrown over it. In fact, if we took a motion picture of a juggler doing the reverse cascade and showed it backwards, it would appear to be a regular cascade. You can learn the reverse cascade by making individual throws from either hand go over the previously thrown object. Then make all the throws from either hand go over the top, and finally combine the two hands in a complete reverse cascade. Avoid making each toss go higher than the previous one. The object should reach its highest point over the hand that threw it, so that it tucks under the next throw.

From the reverse cascade, the logical progression is to the shower. In toss juggling the term shower implies a distinct left-to-right or right-to-left aspect as opposed to the symmetry of cascades. It can refer, as it does here, to a circular pattern that can be used for odd or even numbers of objects, or to doing a trick on every throw, such as showering under the leg or throwing every right-handed throw to a partner in club passing. For these and other juggling terms and definitions, see Larry Weeks' juggling glossary in *Manual of Juggling* by Max Holden. (Chicago: Magic Inc., 1972).

To do the shower, you begin with two balls in your right hand and one in your left. The right hand throws one ball up and to the left in a parabolic trajectory that will drop that ball into your left hand. When this throw reaches the top of its arc, you then throw the remaining ball in your right hand in the exact same arc that the first ball followed. Almost immediately after this second throw, the ball in the left hand is shuffled over laterally into the right hand. If you then catch the first two throws in your left hand, you will have completed a flash of three-ball showering. Once you make a continuum out of it, you will discover that one hand is always throwing upward while the other hand catches these throws and feeds them back into the throwing hand. The catching hand is usually slightly higher, and the hands are held closer together than in the cascade. To do the shower with rings or clubs, the left hand simply slaps the object over to the right hand rather than tossing it; double spins are usually used with clubs as a means of gaining time.

There are many moves with three balls that are predicated on knowing how to do four balls in lanes. The basic move is to juggle two balls in your right hand in lanes while your left hand tosses the third ball up and down in synchronization with the ball in the right lane. The two balls on the outside are being thrown simultaneously while the middle ball rises and falls in counterpoint between them. Although at first the right hand is throwing and catching the middle ball, eventually you should be able to alternate back and forth between both hands. You can also cross the two outside balls by throwing one slightly higher than the other. There are many other variations on this basic two-and-one pattern. For example, instead of actually throwing the ball in your left hand, you can hold it in your hand and create various mime-type illusions. You might just raise and lower it in the same pattern as if you were throwing it, or you might raise and lower it above the middle ball: If the same distance is kept between the two balls, the illusion of a string or magnet may be created.

In addition to varying the direction of the throws, it is just as interesting, if not more so, to alter the position of the arms and body while juggling. A classic example of this would be to juggle with the arms crossed (photo 4.17). I call this the 4,000-year-old trick because it was performed by one of the women depicted in the Egyptian tomb drawings (photo 4.1). When you do this trick, you suddenly enter a new realm of ambidexterity. Juggling while lying on your back or hanging from a trapeze (chapter eight) can be equally disorienting. You might experiment with different patterns: What does it feel like to do a shower or a reverse cascade while on your back with your arms crossed?

Fate and your ability to improvise can play important roles in juggling. For example, if

PHOTO 4.17

you fail to catch one of your throws, you can allow the ball to bounce back into your cascade pattern, making your next throw from the nearest hand and then continuing to juggle as if it were part of the act. If it does not bounce high enough, you can use the bottom of your foot to slap it down so that it bounces back up into your hand. If the floor bounce is intentional, throw the ball higher and then let it drop. It will bounce just that much higher and you can be more sure of it reaching your hands.

You can also allow all three balls to bounce off the floor consecutively by maintaining the same normal cascade rhythm and catching them in the order they were thrown. This idea can then be taken into the realm of floor bouncing, in which case the balls are usually thrown directly down. There are three basic ways of juggling off the floor. The first method is to throw each ball down on the outside so that it bounces up the middle. This is a throwing motion and not just a drop. Each throw has to come all the way back up into your opposite hand. A second method is to shower the balls off the floor. Your right hand sends them down to the same spot on the floor while your left hand catches them and feeds them back into the right hand. The third method involves lifting your hand several inches above the normal level for floor juggling and then releasing the ball down the middle so that it bounces up on the outside. The catches are made with the hands in a palm-down position. The hand is then lifted a few inches and turned sideways so that the ball rolls right off the heel of the hand. This method was originated by the author, who has done as many as seven balls this way.

The slight upward movement of the hand before the ball is released makes the pattern slower and is certainly less strenuous than throwing the balls up in the air.

It is also possible to bounce balls off different parts of the body, such as the knee, elbow, shoulder, forehead and foot. It is generally a good idea to throw the ball fairly low for then the chances of connecting will be much greater and you will be less liable to get bruised.

Objects can also be thrown under the leg or behind the back while juggling. If I am going to throw an object in my right hand under my right leg, I make the throw from my left hand a little higher so I will have time to get my right hand back to catch it. This simple trick already gives us four possiblities on which to work: right throw under right leg, right throw under left leg, left throw under left leg, and left throw under right leg. Throws behind the back have a wide range, including over the same shoulder, over the opposite shoulder, over the head, around the hip or anywhere in between. It is simply a matter of transposing what you did under your leg to behind your back: It helps to make the previous throw a little higher. Throws behind the back are somewhat different with clubs than with balls. You have to get most of the arm behind the back with balls, whereas with clubs this is not necessary because you can choke down on the handle and hold the club by its knob. You may find it easier to throw a club behind your back with a double spin, as this will give you more time. This is especially true if you are making continuous throws behind the back with both hands.

PHOTO 4.18

Since the possibilities with three objects are limitless, it might be interesting to experiment with all the possibilities on your own, using your imagination to the fullest. If you run out of ideas you might seek out a copy of Ken Benge's book, *3-Ball Juggling* (Chicago: Magic Inc., 1972), which is devoted exclusively to variations with three balls.

Mixing objects

A good juggler can juggle almost anything and need not limit himself to balls, rings and sticks. In *The Circus* (United Artists, 1928), Charlie Chaplin is obliged to juggle food. The mean circus owner makes his daughter practice on the Roman rings because she had made a mistake in performance. She is very hungry, and Chaplin is trying to throw a salami, cheese and a roll up to her. She does not catch his first throws and her father walks in while Chaplin is trying to catch the food. To conceal what he is up to, he juggles the roll, cheese and salami for a few throws and then takes a bow. Here it might be interesting for the reader to experiment with different objects so as to determine which group they belong to and how they might be juggled.

Some objects are so abstract and/or adaptable that they can be juggled in more than one way. For example, rings can be juggled in a horizontal plane by flipping them over as if they were linear objects (photo 4.18). Sergei Ignatov has done five rings this way. To juggle amorphous objects such as scarves, you have to claw them out of the air with your knuckles up and grip them as best you can (photo 4.19); you can

PHOTO 4.19

also juggle balls with the hands in an palm-down position. A bucket with a handle transcends the three basic types of objects previously classified. It is thrown end-over-end as if it were a stick, yet it is caught by the handle as if it were a ring (photos 4.20a-i).

Despite the energy shortage, air pollution and the carcinogenic nature of asbestos, fire juggling is still popular with audiences. This can be done with flaming torches (photo 4.21) or with flaming rings (photo 4.22), and Jerry Greenberg even juggles balls of fire while wearing welder's gloves. There is a certain fascination in staring at fire itself, so when combined with juggling, the result is usually super-hypnotic.

Another realm of toss juggling is that of take-aways and formation passing. These involve at least one object being transferred from one juggler to another while juggling.

Take-aways

We can begin with a simple take-away. An "empty-handed" juggler takes away the three balls being cascaded by another juggler. Take-aways can be done with other kinds of objects and with a larger number of objects, but the method for three balls can serve as a model for the more advanced variations.

If you are doing the "stealing" in a three-ball take-away, you stand to the left of your juggling partner (photo 4.23a). Your left hand should be ready to grab the ball that is traveling right to left and your right hand should be poised near your partner's left shoulder so that it can quickly reach across and grab the second ball, which will be

PHOTO 4.20a

PHOTO 4.20b

PHOTO 4.20c

PHOTO 4.20d

PHOTO 4.20e

PHOTO 4.20g

PHOTO 4.20h

PHOTO 4.20f

PHOTO 4.20i

traveling left to right. First intercept a ball that is traveling right to left. Come *above* your partner's left arm so that you do not collide hands; take the ball at the peak of its arc (photo 4.23b). The only thing your partner has to do is to keep his pattern at least shoulder-level high and keep his hands down. As soon as you have caught this first ball, immediately reach across and grab the next ball traveling left to right at the top of its trajectory (photo 4.23c). Because the first ball is moving towards you and the second one away from you, the feeling you get is one of accelerating in order to catch the second throw; in science, this phenomenon is referred to as the Doppler effect. The balls are maintaining the same speed and rhythm, as if they did not know what was going on, but the juggler has to break the rhythm in order to get the second ball. The rhythm of your catches goes 1-2—3, rather than 1—2—3. As you catch the second ball, leave your right elbow raised so that your partner can throw the third ball under your right arm (photo 4.23d). Once the last ball has been thrown, your hands drop to the normal hip level and this third ball is taken into the juggle (photo 4.23e). Take-aways should also be practiced from the right side.

A variation on the take-away is the side-by-side, in which you only take away with the left hand and throw as if your left hand were your partner's. The side-by-side can also be used to teach someone else to juggle. The teacher takes every right-to-left throw from the student, accepting even relatively bad throws, and giving better throws in return. This way the student's right hand is broken

PHOTO 4.21

PHOTO 4.22

PHOTO 4.23a

PHOTO 4.23c

PHOTO 4.23e

PHOTO 4.23b

PHOTO 4.23d

in. Then change sides and break in the left hand by taking the place of the right. The side-by-side also offers comic possibilities. For example, you could replace one object with another. You could just take certain lefts, or run around and take certain rights or back and forth.

One final variation on this is the drop-back: One person juggles three objects and drops them back one at a time (right-left-right) to his partner, who should be standing a few feet behind him and facing the same direction. The drop-back throw is also sometimes used in formation passing.

Double passing

The next step in team juggling is to exchange objects with a partner while both of you are juggling. You do not have to be very advanced with your three-ball cascade to be able to pass six balls with a partner. As long as you can both keep three balls going in an even rhythm, you can pass six between you. Only two balls are being passed at any given time, one by each of you.

As an exercise to learn the throw used in passing, you should begin with three balls and your partner with none. Your partner stands facing you at arm's distance. You start with two balls in your right hand and one in your left. Begin juggling and then throw the fifth throw to your partner. This is the lone ball that started in your left hand and jugglers refer to it as the lead object. The ball should travel straight to your partner, making an arc the same height as your cascade. (After having finally learned to make your juggling

throws in a flat plane in front of you, you may now experience difficulty breaking that plane to throw forward.) Next your partner should throw this ball back to you with his right hand and you should take it back into your left hand, tossing the ball already there over to your right hand so as to continue juggling. Now switch roles with your partner and repeat the same exercise.

Another good preparation for passing is to juggle balls against a wall. Cascade three balls and then throw one of them against a wall arm-distance in front of you so that the ball comes back into your other hand and you continue to juggle. The throw should be at such an angle that it will hit the wall at a point opposite the center of your body and come into your other hand. This should be done with both the right hand and the left hand and can even be done on every throw with both hands at once.

You should now be ready to pass six balls. You and your partner each begin with two balls in the right hand and one in the left. Now you need only add a downbeat in order to start together. A good downbeat is done with your elbows at your sides, your forearms vertical, and your hands at your shoulders. You look into each other's eyes and know when you are going to start (photo 4.24a). You drop the hands to the juggling position and immediately begin to juggle (photo 4.24b). You must juggle in the same rhythm. This involves compromise: If I am going faster (throwing lower) than my partner is, I will slow down (throw higher), or vice versa. You should be juggling at the same height (photo 4.24c). When you get to the fifth throw, you

each throw toward your partner's left shoulder (photo 4.24d). You should try to see beyond your own cascade as much as possible so that you can pick up on your partner's rhythm and also see his shoulder. Once you have made your throw, however, forget about it and look for the ball coming into your left hand: It will soon become apparent to you whether or not your partner caught your throw. You both continue to juggle, catching your partner's throw as if it were your own right-handed throw to yourself. The key ingredient in passing is to make the designated throw in unison. It is a very simple concept. There is nothing random about it, everything is prearranged.

What you have just done is a single pass with the right hand and it is the basis for all passing. If you understand that, you have opened up a whole world for yourself. You might now try to throw every other right hand or even every right hand which, you may recall, is called "showering."

The basic technique explained above also applies to passing clubs. The major difficulty in club passing lies in making a good pass to your partner. This throw is quite different from the throws you are making to yourself as part of the three-club cascade. As the club that is to be passed is caught in your right hand, your hand slides down the handle and grips the club at the knob. The club is swung down and back past your thigh, and then swung forward at arm's length. The club is released before the arm reaches a horizontal position. You do *not* impart spin with your wrist. With practice, the correct amount of spin can be achieved by letting your thumb ride over the knob.

PHOTO 4.24a

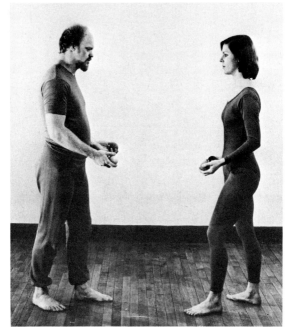

PHOTO 4.24b

PHOTO 4.24c

PHOTO 4.24d

The club is thrown straight across to your partner's left shoulder. He raises his left hand and catches the club, which should arrive in a vertical position with the handle pointing down to the floor. The club has made almost a turn and a half. If it is overturned or underturned and does not arrive in this vertical position, it will be very difficult to catch.

Both partners should practice this throw with just one club until they get the feeling of it. Then do the same exercise with three clubs that you did with three balls (only one partner has three clubs). You will then each know what it is like to pass a club while juggling and to take a club back into your cascade. The final step is to pass six clubs. Club passers usually stand from six to eight feet (1.83-2.44m) apart, but you and your partner should determine what is the most comfortable position for the two of you.

To pass more than six objects with a partner, they must be showered: You pass every throw that comes into a designated hand. To do seven balls, it is simply a matter of one person starting with four and the other with three. Otherwise it is similar to showering six: You make a normal cascade throw from left hand to right and throw every ball that comes into your right hand to your partner's left shoulder. Although it is a little faster and slightly higher, the major difference is that you are throwing in opposition rather than simultaneously.

The person holding four balls (two in each hand) begins by throwing the first ball out of his right hand to his partner's left shoulder. Next he tosses the first ball in his left hand over to his right hand, which he must empty

by passing the ball remaining there over to
his partner. Finally, the remaining ball in his
left hand must be thrown over to his right
hand before the *first* pass from his partner
arrives in his left hand.

The person starting with three balls (two in
the right hand and one in the left) does
almost the same thing he did to pass six. His
first throw is released in the interval between
his partner's first and second passing throw.
All succeeding throws will also be in opposition. If one person can pass with his
left hand, the passes can be made diagonally
so that the pattern becomes a figure-eight.
Seven clubs are usually passed with double
spins (they can be done with singles, but this
is faster).

Before going on to pass eight objects, you
and your partner should practice seven dili-
gently and both know how to start with four.
For eight, the speed will be a little faster and
the arc a little higher, but the only thing different about the approach is that you are both
starting with four and are now once again
throwing simultaneously.

Formation passing

Besides passing six or more objects with a
single partner, there are many interesting
passing formations that require three or more
people. They are done most often with clubs,
but other objects could be substituted. In the
triangle, three jugglers position themselves so
that they form the points of an equilateral
triangle. Each juggler passes in unison to the
person on his right and catches from the
person on his left (photo 4.25).

PHOTO 4.25

PHOTO 4.26

In the *line*, three people stand in a straight line with the two end people facing each other and the middle person facing one of them. The end person who is facing the middle person simply makes a normal, but shorter, pass to him. This middle person does a drop back over his head to the other end person's left hand. This end person in turn does a normal, but longer, pass to the other end person. Throws are made in unison (photo 4.26). The line can be built up in different ways. You might add one or more "drop-back" jugglers, so that you have three or more jugglers facing one direction and one end person facing them. Of course the long throw would then be even longer; the other end person usually has to wait to catch it. The line could also be balanced by adding a juggler to the other side so that there are two jugglers facing in each direction. Each end person receives a drop back from the middle person immediately in front of him and makes a long pass to the more distant middle person. It is also possible to pass more than twelve clubs in a four-person line.

The *feed*, sometimes known as the *teacher*, can be done with three or more people. One juggler (the "teacher") faces two partners who stand next to each other facing the teacher. The teacher showers across to the other two jugglers, alternately feeding each partner. Meanwhile the partners are passing every other (right) back to the teacher. The teacher and first partner would make their first throw on five, but the second partner would not throw until seven, with the partners continuing to take turns passing. It is possible to have the feed take place vertically rather than horizontally by having the teacher feed to the two partners while they are standing in a two-high, feet-to-shoulders (chapter five). This would be called the *two-high feed* (photo 4.27).

It is also possible to do a *two-handed feed* in which the partner on the teacher's left showers right-handedly, the partner on the teacher's right showers left-handedly and the teacher crosses all throws in front of himself with both hands right-handedly to the partner on the left and left-handedly to the partner on his right. During this formation the teacher does not make throws to himself—only passes.

One final formation is called the *box*, although the path of the clubs actually forms a cross. There are two pairs of passing partners—four jugglers in all. They position themselves so that the lines formed by their passes intersect in the middle at right angles to each other. To avoid a collision, the pairs throw every other in counter-time. One pair of partners would start passing on five and the other on seven.

For the *showering box*, in which all four jugglers shower, it is necessary for one pair to start with two clubs in the left hand while the other pair starts with two clubs in the right. By using the same downbeat, the right-handed throws of the two pairs of jugglers are automatically put in counter-time, and collisions in the center can be avoided. There are also hexagonal (with six jugglers) and octagonal (with eight jugglers) versions of the box.

PHOTO 4.27

In stack equilibristics, the performer balances atop some animate or inanimate support that is portable, freely moving and potentially unstable. Such bases of support are usually constituted from three general categories. They are either rolling devices (rola-bola, rolling globe, cycles), stilting devices (stilts, unsupported ladder) or other animate beings. Practical application of these skills frequently arises in everyday life.

I introduce my students to stack equilibristics by teaching them to balance on a rola-bola, walk on stilts and stand on my shoulders. Careful attention is paid to learning these representative skills as correctly as possible. This experience provides a frame of reference that, through comparison and contrast, can make the rest of the work safer and more comprehensible.

Rola-bola

A rola-bola consists simply of a cylinder and a board. The board is placed across the cylinder, the feet are placed on the board and you try to balance there. The rola-bola is its generic name, but it has also been manufactured commercially in a slightly modified form under the trade name "Bongo Board," a patent for which (U.S. patent no. 2,764,411) was issued to Stanley Washburn, Jr., September 25, 1956. This version is popular among skiers who use it to improve their lateral balance during pre-season conditioning. It even appeared in the centerfold of *Playboy* magazine in August, 1967.

The rola-bola need not be dangerous, but it can be if you fail to remember one thing: Always keep *both* feet on the board! You are

5

Stack equilibristics

not likely to get hurt if you keep both feet on the board and just ride it down to the left or to the right when you lose your balance. People have a very strong tendency to take their foot away without even consciously intending to do so because they confuse this with a different kind of balancing. If you take your foot away, there are all sorts of unpleasant possibilities. You might have your legs thrown out from under you as if you had slipped on ice or on a banana peel—and if you land on that cylinder you risk being injured by it. You could also send the board across the room and injure somebody else, or the board might catapult you across the room. So keep both feet on the board! I advise my students not to even so much as go up on their toes in their struggle to maintain balance. If your center of gravity is off to the side, no amount of kicking or throwing your legs in the air is going to help. There is a small zone where you can lose and regain your balance, but it is very small. It is similar to kicking up into a handstand (chapter two): If your center of gravity is altogether in the wrong place. you have to come down and try again.

I usually spot my students on their first attempts by watching their torsos and guiding them back to center if they get out of line. I also watch their feet out of the corner of my eye. If a foot starts to come off the board I prepare to catch them, slow down their fall or, at the very least, keep them from landing upside down. To learn it on your own, all you need is a wall. You should be close enough to the wall to be able to hold it without leaning forward and putting too much weight on the toes. At the same time, you want to be far

enough from the wall so that it will not interfer with your rolling. I have found one foot (30.48 cm) to be a good distance. Hold the wall with both hands—it would be even easier if you had a railing to grip. The cylinder should be centered under the board so that you always begin at the same convenient angle no matter which side you start from (photo 5.1a). Push or pull equally with both hands. because if you push with one hand and pull with the other, you will tend to spin around (photo 5.1b). Some people take their hands away and then struggle until they lose their balance. It might be better to let go of the wall, but then grab it before you completely lose your balance (photo 5.1c). Once you get the feel of it, you will not need the wall at all, but in the meantime it will save you a lot of wasted time spent setting up the board and cylinder and getting on it. Give yourself the benefit of the doubt, not as an equilibrist, but as a person in need of assistance.

The board's range of movement to the left and to the right is greater than most people imagine. The outside range of extremes comes to about twice the length of the board plus the circumference of the cylinder. If you practice alongside someone else, be sure to allow enough room to avoid collisions. If you are using a 32-inch (81.28 cm) board and a 6-inch (15.24 cm) diameter cylinder. the space needed would be at least 75 inches (190.5 cm).

There are two basic movements that can take place on the board. It can teeter like a seesaw on the shifting fulcrum formed by its contact with the cylinder, or it can roll from

PHOTO 5.1a

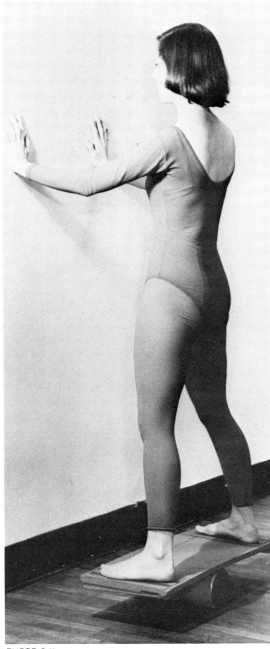

side to side like a pinion and rack, with the board staying parallel to the floor. Generally you will use a combination of both movements, but from time to time one or the other may predominate. For successful work there should not be very much lunging; it is more of a swinging and swaying or rocking and rolling movement. Your center of gravity, head and spine should stay in place, while your legs go from side to side, compensating for the rolling movement (photos 5.2a-c). The magnitude of the swing should be moderate at first. Some performers greatly exaggerate the movement for effect, but if you have good control, you can also render the movement barely perceptible. It could look as though you were just standing on it, but of course you will never be absolutely still any more than your hand would be when balancing a cue stick.

Despite the common tendency to do so, it is not a good idea to look at the board, especially if you want to juggle, relate to an audience or support another person on top of you. Unless the board is transparent, you will not have a good view of the cylinder's movement anyway. About all you would see is a moving board, and that will not tell you anything because you are moving with it. Look straight ahead and focus on a point at eye level, whether you are facing a wall in front of you or looking clear across a room. Try to feel the balance and sense where the cylinder is. Since you want the upper part of your body to remain fixed, you need a fixed point to relate to. You have no such point of reference when you look at the board. To toss juggle on the rola-bola, your gaze focuses on your jug-

PHOTO 5.1b

PHOTO 5.1c

 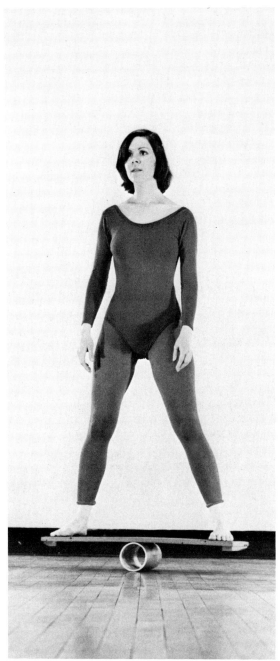 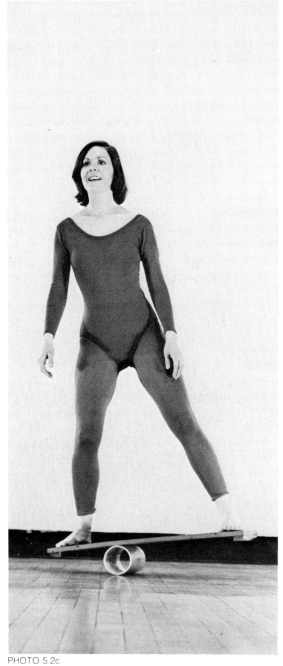

PHOTO 5.2a

PHOTO 5.2b

PHOTO 5.2c

gling pattern just as you begin to juggle and then quickly switches back to a more distant point, at the same eye level, the instant you stop juggling.

Stilts

The use of stilts goes back very far and is fairly common throughout the world. They have been used for occupational, recreational, theatrical and ritualistic purposes. Stilts play a prominent role in many African dances and archeological excavations have uncovered prehistoric evidence of stilt-walking. In the Marquesas Islands in the South Pacific and in Les Landes, a marshy region in France, stilts are used to walk over damp or flooded lands. In 1891, Silvain Dornon, a resident of Les Landes, walked on stilts from his hometown to Moscow, covering the more than 2,000 miles (3,218 km) in only 58 days. Today, aluminum stilts are used by builders, bricklayers, house painters, fruit farmers and hop pickers so they can work at high, fixed levels and still move around.

Walking on hand stilts is similar to balancing a cue stick in that the top should not move as much as the base does. You might even try balancing a stilt on your hand to see what is involved. Since you always have two stilts, you are constantly changing from one to the other. The stilt comes straight up your side and is held right against your shoulder blade: It is very important not to let it move away from your shoulder blade because, unlike a cue stick, you cannot see where it is—you must feel where it is. You grip each stilt with the back of your hands out to the side and your thumbs in front. If you keep your thumbs in front, you know without looking down that you have a place for your feet. I have seen people rotate the stilt after they get up and then wonder why the step is in the wrong position to hold them up.

To learn to mount the stilts, it may be preferable to find someone to hold them for you. You step up as if you were climbing onto a ladder. Then bring your arms into position. If your hands are straight down, it can be difficult to hold the stilts against the shoulders. If your hands are way up high, it can be uncomfortable. Therefore, you should probably have about a 60° angle at the elbow, or whatever gives you the best triangulation for the two parts of your arm and the part of the stilt between your shoulder and hand.

As soon as you are leaning slightly forward, your friend can let go of the stilts and you can start walking. It is important *not* to take either foot off the stilts. As you step, you lift with the same arm. This is not very natural: Normally you move your arms in opposition to your legs. Here you swing your right arm and right leg at the same time and vice versa. (This gait is natural for camels, but then I have never seen a camel walk on stilts.)

In an effort to make sure that their feet do not slide off the stilts, some beginners push outward when they step so the stilts fail to remain parallel. If you do this, be sure to compensate with your arms. If the base of the stilts is wider than your shoulders, they will become A-shaped and no longer be parallel. If the stilts were made to accommodate a taller person, they might even become X-shaped and clip together at the top.

Before you can step, you have to lean forward or you will fall backward. You can lean forward a little bit and take small slow steps. You can lean forward quite a bit and take either long slow steps or rapid small steps. It is neither advisable nor likely that you will lean forward so much that you will have to take rapid long steps. The greater danger is that you will not lean forward far enough, will take moderate steps at a moderate speed, and still overtake your forward lean. If you should strike a perfect balance, stop and wait until you fall forward a little bit before taking additional steps.

You should avoid crossing steps. When your weight is on the right foot, your lean should be forward and to the left so that once you place the stilt you will land on it. It is very important to be relaxed. Your walk can be quite natural and normal. Do not crouch over or lock your knees. If you know how to dance, you could even try dancing on stilts when you become proficient.

Although it is not impossible, it is extremely difficult to balance on the stilts without moving and with weight on both feet. Normally, you are shifting your weight completely from one stilt to the other. This is true even if you are standing in place. The only time your weight should be equally divided between your two feet is when you are going to jump.

If you want to get up on the stilts without help, you can use steps or similar elevation. If you do, be sure not to put the bottom ends of the stilts way out in front of you or you may fall back onto the steps. The closer the base of the stilts are, the better chance there is of pitching yourself far enough forward to achieve the necessary forward lean.

There is also a fairly simple way to mount if you must do it without any external support whatsoever. Hold the stilts in the proper arm position, but with your hands a bit lower because you are not yet up. Take one foot and stretch it right up onto the step (photo 5.3a). Have the stilt as vertical as possible, but have some bend in your other knee. From there you jump up (photo 5.3b) and pitch your body forward so as to get both feet in position (photo 5.3c). If you are leaning forward, start walking. If you are too far forward to start walking, then you simply went too far. If you fall to the back, you did not go far enough. What you are aiming for is a slightly forward position. Wait for the right moment to take the first step; from there, you may walk a step or two in this crouched position and then slide up to a normal position. Do not grip the stilt too tightly, because you are going to slide your arms up with your body (photo 5.3d).

The best way to get down from stilts is to plié as you land without letting go of them (photo 5.3e). People do have a tendency to drop the stilts, but you should try to hold them, particularly if you are around other people. If you fall to the front or the back, there is no serious problem in landing on your feet. A fall to the side would be more of a problem, but the only way this would happen would be if you placed your right stilt to the left of your center of gravity or vice versa.

PHOTO 5.3a

PHOTO 5.3b

PHOTO 5.3c

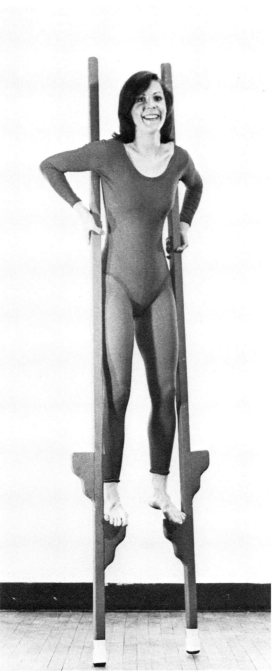

PHOTO 5.3d

PHOTO 5.3e

Two-high, feet-to-shoulders

All human columns and pyramids, including the two-high, feet-to-shoulders, involve people being stacked on other people. Like the take-aways and passing that were part of toss juggling (chapter four), this too enters into the realm of circus teamwork. And since there is the ever-present danger of the top-mounter falling from the shoulders of the understander and being injured, successful teamwork becomes critically important. This is the first time in this book that we encounter this sort of mutual responsibility, but it will now play an increasingly important role, particularly in rigging equilibristics (chapter eight) and catapult vaulting (chapter nine).

I have often found it necessary to instill a sense of concern for others in my students. It is never sufficient just to mention it; it has to be learned. I have to find out who can be trusted and who cannot. Some circus techniques require a very professional attitude, and sometimes students just cannot relate to this circus sense of responsibility. Although teamwork does impose certain risks, it also produces some of the most exciting acts in the circus. It can also make the people involved feel very close to each other. When you trust someone else with your life, a sense of intimacy, even of family, usually develops, without necessarily any sexual connotations whatsoever. In fact, this kind of teamwork can be far more exciting than having sexual relations with someone because you are risking more. Also, I have found that acting students who perform circus well together al-so work well together in acting scenes.

In any human column, there is an understander who supports the weight of the top-mounter. The simplest and most familiar example of a two-high is riding piggyback (photo 5.4) or sitting on someone's shoulders (seat-to-shoulders) (photo 5.5).

In my classes, I begin with the two-high; but since I myself am the understander for all my students, the situation may be quite different from explaining it here. Eventually the students learn to take the weight of their fellow students upon themselves so that the teacher does not have to be the understander indefinitely. In a way, the two-high requires that one of the two people have experience in it. If both people are inexperienced, it is not likely that they are going to be able to figure it out. If I have an experienced top-mounter and an inexperienced understander, I use them together in the mechanic (photo 8.1) with myself on the ropes as the spotter. (Students could also be taught to use a mechanic; in the Moscow Circus School all students must learn to spot with a mechanic.) So although I do think the two-high ought to be learned with an experienced teacher, I can at least write about some of the principles involved.

The understander assumes a wide stance and makes a deep plié with his spine relatively straight. The lower his hips and shoulders, the easier it is going to be for the top-mounter to get up. This also puts the thighs in a more horizontal position. The top-mounter stands to the rear of the understander and they hold hands above the understander's shoulders. This should be a firm handshake, with right hand in right hand

PHOTO 5.4

PHOTO 5.5

and left in left. The top-mounter places her right foot on the understander's right thigh (photo 5.6a): The foot should be right next to the hip, otherwise it may slide down. Then the top-mounter immediately places her left foot on the understander's left shoulder (photo 5.6b). She then steps right in next to the neck (but not on the hair). (Do *not* step on the outside of the understander's shoulders because you will put pressure on the arm where it joins the shoulder and this can result in bursitis.) This step up to the left shoulder is the only difficult part of the mounting. Even if the understander is crouched low, to go from the floor to the shoulder in one step is quite a stretch. But if you can get that foot on the shoulder and the knee over it, it is not hard to straighten the leg and get all the way up. It is extremely important for the understander to raise his arm up as the foot goes on to his shoulder. The other arm goes up as the top-mounter straightens that leg. The understander's hands should never be wider than shoulder distance. It is very easy for the top-mounter to pull the understander backward when she starts climbing up: She must stand close and take her weight right up over the understander.

As soon as the left foot is in position, the top-mounter simply straightens up her left leg and brings her right leg onto the understander's right shoulder (photo 5.6c). The heels and knees should be close together. The understander releases the top-mounter's left hand and grips her left calf just below the knee (photo 5.6d), and then does the same thing on the right side (photo 5.6e). The

PHOTO 5.6a

PHOTO 5.6b

PHOTO 5.6c

PHOTO 5.6d

PHOTO 5.6e

70 Circus techniques

top-mounter's knees, calves and heels should be together, pushing forward on the back of the understander's head, while the understander pushes back against the top-mounter's calves with his head. Unless the understander's hands have to be free, as for juggling, he also pulls the top-mounter's calves against the back of his head. This bond between the top-mounter's calves and the understander's head is the key to the two-high, feet-to-shoulders (photo 5.7). The top-mounter's ankles should never straddle or clamp around the understander's head. The top-mounter remains relaxed and relatively immobile while the understander does most of the balancing.

As the top-mounter's center of gravity passes the understander's head, the understander changes his stance. Initially the stance is lateral, but this is not as strong as it could be because it provides very little forward-back stability. If the understander had one leg right in front of the other, it would be equally unstable, although this time from side to side. However, with the left leg forward and the right leg back, and shoulder-distance between them, you can create a situation which is stable left to right, forward and back, and in one direction diagonally.

Supporting someone like this is a very personal thing. No two shoulders are the same to stand on and no two top-mounters feel the same on your shoulders. The same person feels the same each time if the two-high is being performed correctly, but no two people feel the same.

The inexperienced understander sometimes does crazy things. He may leave his arms

PHOTO 5.7

near his shoulders instead of going up with the top-mounter. If he does go up with her, he may bring his arms too far out in front or too far apart. He tends to hold the ankles, which is a mistake; he should hold behind the knees. He tends to collapse. Although the understander can usually hold the legs, he must also know when to let the top-mounter jump down and land on her feet if he loses the balance. It is up to the top-mounter to come down feet first, but it is up to the understander not to make that impossible by holding the legs too long. What can happen with unsupervised beginners is that they get up there with the understander holding his partner's ankles, the top-mounter yells, "Hey, I'm falling," and the understander says, "Don't worry, I've got you." The result can be disastrous, because the inexperienced understander may cause the top-mounter to land on her head by holding her legs.

If the top-mounter loses her balance to the back, she should jump down and reach for the understander because the understander cannot reach for her; she sort of slides down the understander's back, as it were. If the top-mounter comes down the front, the understander grabs her wherever he can hold on. You should try to avoid falling to the side because it makes it considerably harder to get your feet under yourself.

If you wish to try the two-high without a mechanic, have at least two spotters. They should be placed at a moderate distance behind the two-high at about 45° angles. If the top-mounter goes off the front, the understander spots her. If she falls straight back, both spotters can reach her and do what is necessary. If she does fall to one side, the spotter on that side is responsible for her. (In the incredible five-man-highs performed by some teeterboard troupes, people are dropping all over the place if they miss but somebody is always there to catch them; someone gets between them and the floor.)

If the top-mounter is dismounting of her own free will, and not falling off, she could sit on the understander's shoulders, hold hands and then have the understander go down on his knees and place her flat on the ground. If she is not afraid to jump, the understander releases the right calf and takes the right hand (photo 5.8a), and then does the same thing on the other side (photo 5.8b). The top-mounter jumps forward, keeping her arms straight as the understander offers resistance (photo 5.8c) and pliés upon impact.

Basic principles

It is by plan, not accident or coincidence, that I have placed stack equilibristics at the center of this book. Indeed, they are at the center of circus techniques. Except when flying or falling we are always in some state of equilibrium, however stable or precarious, as long as we are within the gravitational field of the earth. Thus other circus techniques are mutually compatible with stack equilibristics. You may juggle (chapters one, four and seven) in states of stack equilibrium, and you may vault (chapters three, six and nine) to and from states of stack equilibrium. You can even combine inverted equilibristics (chapter two) or rigging equilibristics (chapter eight) with stack equilibristics.

PHOTO 5.8a

PHOTO 5.8b

PHOTO 5.8c

Double rola-bola

A most interesting progression is to place one cylinder across the top of another cylinder. They are both rolling surfaces and the bottom one is placed along the long axis of the board, while the top one rolls in the normal manner (photo 5.9). The board can go every which way, so of course the dangers involved here become much greater than with the single rola-bola.

When I do it, I usually have two people hold the four corners of the board while I hold their heads in order to get up. I have them take their hands away, and when I feel pretty comfortable, I remove my hands from their heads and have them run away. If I am assisting someone who is doing it, I stand in front of them—but I also make sure I have my steel-toed shoes on. The person going up holds my hands.

When I am all by myself, I use a railing for this, but it is still very difficult to get up. I place the two cylinders across each other and the board on top and then try to hold it all in place with one foot in the middle of the board. I then plié deeply on the other foot and try to jump up and land with both feet on the board. The foot that was on the floor goes to one end and the foot that was on the middle of the board lands on the opposite end—both with equal weight. I am still holding the railing; when I feel comfortable up there, I take my hands away.

The movements required to balance on two cylinders can vary somewhat. Since the distance from one foot to the other is approxi-

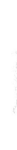

PHOTO 5 9

mately three times as great as that from toe to heel. you can figure on making three times as much side-to-side movement as forward and back movement. When I balance on two cylinders, I feel like I am describing an ellipse, but it is a very small movement. If one corner of the board starts to go up, I have to apply more weight there; the feet steer the board with pressure from the heels and toes. I try to establish a little rhythm. The actual movement through space is very small. All I try to do is keep that board horizontal.

I have heard of someone doing three cylinders, rolling surface to rolling surface (bottom and top parallel), but I have never seen it done. What is usually seen is the insertion of one or more upright cylinders—this has gone as high as five cylinders. There is one vertical cylinder between each rolling surface, so the order is vertical, rolling, vertical, rolling, vertical. The build-up to five cylinders usually catches the imagination of the audience, but the progression is not what it seems to be. Only one or two cylinders are rolling. This has been performed in the Moscow Circus by many performers, including clown-mime Leonid Yengibarov.

Rolling globe

The rolling globe is simply a large sphere that you can try to balance or even walk on. It is a direct extension of the rola-bola. People's instincts on this are usually pretty good, and many animals have learned to do it, particularly bears. However, the rolling globe can be very dangerous if you let yourself get caught in the wrong position. If the ball starts to roll

PHOTO 5.10

forward so that your toes lift off and you find yourself supported on your heels, your feet may fall out from under you and you may fall on the globe. And once you find yourself in that position, there is nothing you can do about it. You must not fall off the front! This could injure you. Always be ready to bail out sideways or backwards. Your spotter should always watch your hips, and if they go forward he should immediately grab you.

Stand on the globe with your feet forming two sides of a square (photo 5.10). If the globe rolls to the side, push, with the heel and toe of the opposite foot. If the ball starts to roll forward. push with your heels. Do *not* lift your foot off. Make the globe move like a rola-bola, that is from side to side. Imagine that it is on rails and roll it side to side along these ''rails.'' It is far more difficult to balance forward and back than it is to balance side to side. For example, if a mime imitates a tightrope walker, he can indicate great difficulty by standing sideways on the imaginary rope so that the loss of balance is front and backward bodily. While you initiate a sideways movement, also stay on the brink of going backwards, then at least you can bend your knees and land on your feet with your hands on top of the ball. You do not risk injuring yourself as you would if you fell off the front.

Unicycle

The unicycle usually consists of a single wheel twenty inches (50.8 cm) (photo 5.11) or twenty-four inches (60.96 cm) (photo 5.12) in diameter, two pedals and pedal shanks, a fork and a seat. It creates its own rolling situ-

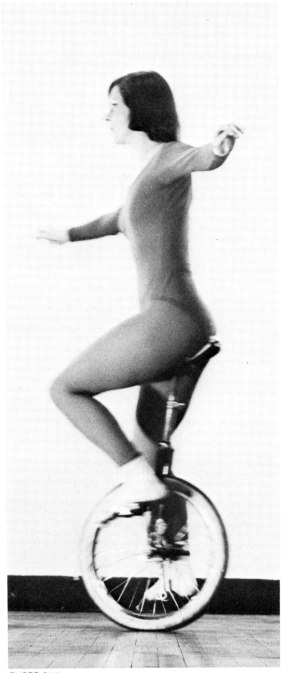

PHOTO 5.11

PHOTO 5.12

ation, but it is also more complicated than the rola-bola or the rolling globe. Because of the unusual combination of fork and wheel, the unicycle is a cross between a rolling and a stilting device.

The unicycle is a very individual thing. It does not really lend itself to team work the way some of the other circus activities do. It is "uni"—almost a soloist field. You can of course join hands and do formations. You can help a student just so much with a unicycle. He really has to learn it by himself.

The first step is to achieve a full cycle of the wheel. It seems slow in the beginning, because every inch you go is a new position to learn to balance in. Once you learn to go that first cycle of the wheel, however, each succeeding cycle is the same. Some people learn to balance for that first five feet (1.52 m) or so only to discover that they can then ride fifty feet (15.24 m) or more. So there is a payoff for those who will stick it out until they can go the circumference of the wheel without any assistance.

The fork does not really have to be vertical, and can even be slightly back if your body is leaning slightly forward. If you imagine a plumb line passing through the unicycle axle, then your shoulders should be in front of that line and your hips behind it. This will give you the forward lean that makes it possible to go forward. But if the wheel gets in front or in back of that plumb line, you will lose your balance.

Mount the unicycle by holding on to other people or a wall or railing. Grab the seat of the unicyle with one hand and your support with the other. Engage the lower pedal with your foot centered on it so that you can push either with your toe or heel. One of the most common mistakes is to put your weight on the pedal that is up. This will not work! You *must* put your foot on the pedal that is down.

You now swing up onto the seat with your other foot coming to rest on the top pedal. However, if you now push down while one pedal is directly up and the other is directly down, you have absolutely no assurance that you are going to go forward, and you may well go backwards. The only way you can be sure a downward push is going to take you forward is to move the top pedal a number of degrees forward. The best point for applying pressure downward so as to go forward would be when the top pedal is about 45° from the zenith. You then pedal forward, exerting the force for 90° and then letting it coast for the other 90°, so that you now have the other pedal in a good starting position. Another 180° turn will give you a full cycle. This is what you want to achieve without any assistance and you can only do it with practice.

The time you put into practicing the unicycle can be free of injuries if you just take a few precautions. I have found that the ankle area because of its thin skin is quite vulnerable to cutting. If you are using a good unicycle, there will be bolts that can cut this area, so it is best to pad the ankles before you begin practicing. Just take a piece of athletic training tape and fold it over into several squares, place it over the inside of your ankle, and then wrap it around. Do not apply it too tightly: You should still be able to point and flex the foot. Do this anytime you

attempt a new trick on the unicycle. You *could* pad the unicycle, but you would be covering up bolts that forever need tightening.

You should experience no real problems in falling from a twenty-inch (50.8 cm) or twenty-four-inch (60.96 cm) unicycle. You land on your right foot if you fall to the right and on your left foot if you fall to the left. You can land on both feet if you fall to the front or back. If you do fall off the front or back, it is better to grab the seat as you come down. If you let your unicycle hit the ground too often, you will end up with a damaged unicycle.

If you are falling backwards, there is a slight tendency for your feet to go flying up into the air. If this should happen, be sure that your fingers are pointing in the *same* direction as your legs when you put your hands back to cushion your fall, for otherwise you may sprain your wrist. (This applies to *all* falls.)

Once you can ride the unicycle a short distance you should learn to mount it without any assistance. The approach can be substantially the same as before, but without any support to hold onto, the action of stepping up will tend to swivel your body around. Push to the left with your right leg as you swing your left leg up. As you jump forward to get on, you will be putting pressure on the top pedal with your foot, which should move the pedal past the zenith to a good starting position. Do not let go of the seat until you get up there. Let your weight fall forward ever so slightly and then begin to pedal.

Making turns on the unicycle can be done in either of two ways. You can actually twist the unicycle while the wheel stays per-

pendicular to the ground, or you can lean into the turn by banking the unicycle. This will allow you to turn in a smooth arc, as you would on a bicycle.

You might learn to ride backwards and idle (rock back and forth) at about the same time, but if you do not have any sense of going backwards, then it is of course hard to idle. Once you learn to idle, you can work more on riding backwards. You generally idle with one foot down. The number of degrees from the vertical must be the same to both the front and the back. You can lift the other leg off while rocking, and it is even possible to ride a unicycle with one foot: You re-exert the force by doing a vertical loop with the single foot. To learn to ride backwards, you might try holding hands with someone who is going forward. It is even better if there are three of you. The two going forward hold a pole between them while the third person holds onto it in front of him as he pedals backwards.

You can of course juggle while riding a unicycle. I find it a lot easier to travel forward while juggling than to rock back and forth in place. However, idling does have the advantage of freeing one leg so you can lift it or throw underneath it during a forward swing of the body and backward swing of the leg.

There are many variations on the unicycle, including a midget unicycle, which can be a lot of fun to use. There is even a motorized one, the "Weelie" (U.S. patent no. 3,399,742), invented by Frank Malick. The most common variation is the high unicycle, usually called a "giraffe," (photo 5.13). The pedals drive the wheel by means of a chain, but the gear ratio

PHOTO 5.13

is 1:1. Any chain-driven unicycle must be at least the radius of the wheel higher than an ordinary unicycle, for otherwise your pedals would be in the spokes. The only commercially-made model has a twenty-inch (50.8 cm) wheel and a single chain.

A giraffe is easier to balance on because the distance you have to fall before you realize you are off balance is very small. This gives you plenty of time to do something about it. It is, however, a good idea to be able to go backwards and to idle on the low unicycle before you attempt the higher model. If you have mastered the low unicycle, you can master the giraffe. The only difficulty is psychological.

The main danger with the high unicycle is falling laterally. If you fall to the right or left, you cannot land on your foot in the same way you would if you were falling off a normal unicycle. If you try to jump free of the unicycle, you will probably get tangled up in it, so it may be preferable to land on your side, but this can also injure you. The best approach is to avoid lateral falls by taking greater risks of falling backwards and forward. When you fall to the front or the back, you do not really pivot on the wheel. The wheel actually rolls out from underneath you and you go straight down. You ride the unicycle down to a certain degree, so it is a bit slower than a normal fall. As always, do not forget to plié on impact.

A giraffe can be mounted from a ladder, but it is also possible to climb up without assistance. You place one foot on top of the wheel to keep it from rolling. You then place your other foot on the low pedal and step up into a sitting position.

A classic trick is to ride a circus bicycle (1:1 gear ratio; no coaster brakes) as if it were a unicycle. The bicycle is tipped up on the rear wheel and pedals in that position (photo 5.14). Since the front wheel is forward, you can be leaning back in this trick and still be in a forward balance. You feel tipped back but are usually too far forward. However, since it is easier to dismount forward and more dangerous to go off the back, you should always stay on the brink of falling forward.

Advanced stilt-walking

If you are using stilts with two levels of steps, you can turn each stilt 180° and climb onto the higher steps while in balance. To do so, you switch over one stilt at a time. Since you are turning each stilt 180°, you have to "wind up" your hand for the turn. In the normal position, your thumb is in the front. You bring your thumb to the outside and work your fingertips to the inside (photo 5.15a). As you step up, turn the stilt 180° to the inside (photo 5.15b). This puts your thumb on the inside and your fingers on the outside. Now work your thumb back to the front and your fingers back to the inside. You do not actually rise up on the first turn because your weight is still on the other stilt. Now do the same wind-up with the other hand (photo 5.15c). When you change steps on the second stilt (photo 5.15d), you straighten your first leg in order to lift up your body and second leg (photo 5.15e).

PHOTO 5.14

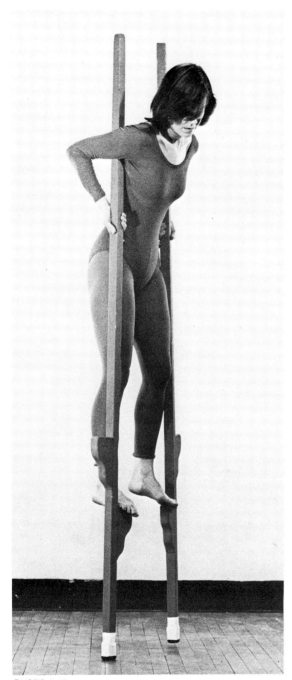

PHOTO 5.15a

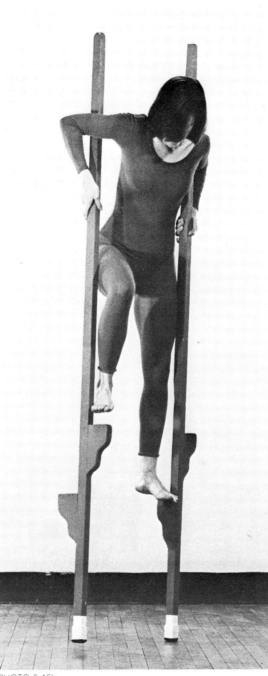

PHOTO 5.15b

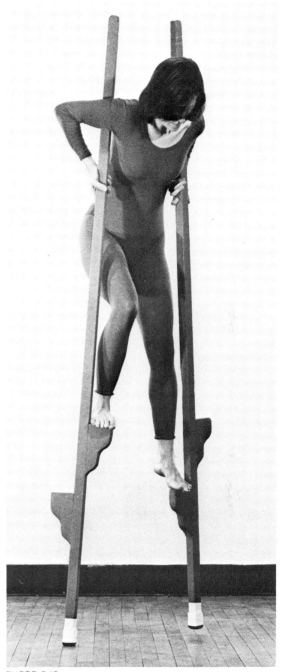

PHOTO 5.15c

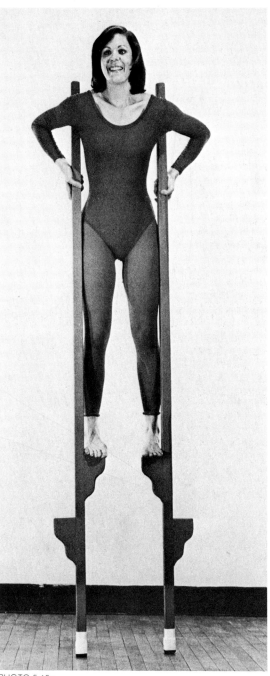

The major difference between lower and higher levels is psychological. In terms of body mechanics, you have leverage at your foot and, in another sense, at your hand. The ratio of the shoulder-to-foot distance to the foot-to-floor distance has a direct bearing on the amount of strength you need. And the strength it takes to hold those stilts against the shoulders will affect your control. The dynamics of the balance is easier because of the height, but when you are slightly off balance and have to strain to hold the stilts, high stilts become harder.

For a softer landing from high stilts, do a knee bend, slide your hands down, jump off, straighten your legs in the air and then do another plié as you land. This will lower your center of gravity, so you have less effective distance to drop. Generally you should not go any higher than you feel you can safely come down from.

Instead of holding the stilts behind your shoulders, you can also walk holding the stilt stile in front of your shoulders (photo 5.16). This is less efficient because it requires more strength: Your fist must be kept at a constant fixed point in front of your shoulders. This method, however, is an intermediate step toward stilts à la pogo stick and unsupported ladder. This method is also used in the Orient where the "bamboo horse" stilts made of bamboo have a step attached to the back of the stilt.

After you learn to walk on stilts by holding them in front of your shoulders, I think the pogo stilt would be the next logical progression. This "pogo stilt" is like a pogo stick, except there is no spring to give you

PHOTO 5.15d

PHOTO 5.15e

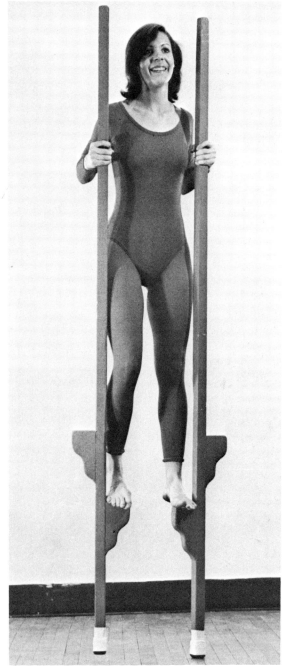

PHOTO 5.16

an extra lift. It is all done with your own energy. You might prepare for it by jumping while on both stilts so you get a sense of parallelism. Then if there are steps on each side of a single stilt, with both steps at the same height, you can jump up and down on a single stilt (photo 5.17). This is not particularly difficult. You could even do it with the steps attached at different levels or using only one foot. The major problem is that the stile gets in your way and can even injure you.

Unsupported ladder

You can also balance and walk on an unsupported ladder as if it were a pair of stilts. However, it may have to be reinforced with braces so that it withstands the twisting and turning it takes to balance on it. The unsupported ladder is an extension of stilt-walking, but this does not mean that everybody who does unsupported ladder arrived in this manner. It would be valuable to first learn to walk on hand stilts by holding them in front of you, because this is how you hold the ladder. The difference is that when you are walking forward with the stilts, you can go directly forward with one stilt and then with the other. When you walk on the unsupported ladder (photo 5.18), you must pivot on the stile you are supported on in order to walk forward with the other one. In order to get the weight off one stile and on to the other, you have to tip the whole ladder slightly over to the side.

Buster Keaton does a "flash" of unsupported ladder in his movie *One Week* (Metro Pictures Corporation, 1920). He is building a

PHOTO 5.17

PHOTO 5.18

house and uses the bannister from the front porch as a ladder. As he comes down the ladder it tips away from the house to a vertical position. While the ladder balances there completely unsupported, Keaton steps around to the other side, whereupon the ladder falls back against the house. To avoid making the same mistake he walks down the inside of the ladder.

Strap-on stilts

Strap-on stilts are strapped tightly to your legs but are not held by the hands or supported by the shoulders. They are dangerous if you fall because you obviously cannot land on your feet. The pelvis is especially vulnerable. If you do fall, the best you can hope for is to roll over on your side on impact. The dangers are even greater if you are using very tall stilts.

Your body balances in a somewhat bowed position. Your shoulders are over the bottom ends of the stilts with the rest of your weight slightly behind the stilts. This puts the stress on the back of the knee, which locks into place. Be careful to keep the supporting leg straight. Your stance can be a little wider than shoulder width and the stilts do not have to be parallel (photo 5.19).

Strap-on stilts are most commonly seen worn under a pair of very long pants to create the illusion of the wearer being very tall. It is very much a part of parades and circus production numbers. There are, however, many other possibilities. The Dovyeko act featured a back somersault on stilts from the teeterboard (chapter nine).

PHOTO 5.19

Advanced human columns

The two-high, feet-to-shoulders is the basis for most human columns. It can be extended into three-high and four-high columns or the base can be widened to form triangular pyramids. The understander could sit or lie down or the top-mounter could balance on him in an upside-down position (chapter two). The balance does not have to be feet-to-shoulders. It could be feet-to-feet, feet-to-hands, hands-to-hands, head-to-head, hands-to-feet, etc. It could be just a single hand or foot. You might even insert a perch pole (chapter eight) between the understander and top-mounter. It then becomes more like balance juggling (chapter one) for the understander and rigging equilibristics (chapter eight) for the top-mounter. There are so many possibilities; your imagination can come up with variations faster than you can learn the techniques for them.

A simple example of a variation would be the thigh stand (photo 5.20), which can be arrived at quite simply from a seat-to-shoulders position (photo 5.5). Another attitude is the arch (photo 5.21), which is also used in dance. The foot-to-shoulder arabesque is an advanced variation of the two-high, feet-to-shoulders. In addition to holding the calf at the back, the understander places his other hand on the front of the same knee, bracing that leg sufficiently for her to take her other leg off his shoulder and strike the arabesque (photo 5.22).

These partner equilibristics are often referred to as "adagio." Technically speaking,

PHOTO 5.20

PHOTO 5.21

PHOTO 5.22

they are not adagio unless the movements are performed slowly, but in the circus the term has lost much of its original meaning. Often an adagio duo will do a series of slow moves to music, combining dance with equilibristics. There is also the quartet adagio made up of three men and one woman. Usually two men specialize in throwing the woman—one for each side—and the other in catching her (see chapter nine). Today the term "team acrobatics" is becoming more common and is probably more accurate.

Another possibility is to take these columns into the realm of inverted equilibristics. The simplest inverted two-high that two people can do is no harder than a headstand and probably a lot easier. The understander lies on his back with his knees up, feet on the floor and arms raised. The top-mounter grasps the knees of the understander and stretches her arms out straight, leaning forward until her shoulders are resting in his hands. She then kicks up into an inverted balance and the understander supports her shoulders simply by keeping his arms straight (photo 5.23). The top-mounter has a broad base of support. She can come down the way she went up. If the top-mounter overbalances forward, the understander should push up on her shoulders so that she can land on her feet.

Other examples of inverted columns would be a progression away from this simple stunt, such as the top-mounter taking her hands away from the understander's knees and grasping his arms instead (low arm-to-arm). This could eventually lead to a high hand-to-hand handstand. My favorite example of an

PHOTO 5.23

inverted column was performed by a brother and sister in the Hai Chia acrobatic troupe from Taiwan. He balanced in a free headstand on his sister's head for at least five minutes. During this time, they both drank, ate and smoked. In order to light his cigarette, she took him in a hand-to-hand (handstand) and lowered him down momentarily so her cigarette lit his.

The understander could also lie on his back and support another person on his feet. I have seen fathers do this with their children. The understander lies on his back, preferably with some support under his hips, and places his hands on the floor (palms up) near his shoulders. The top-mounter stands on the understander's hands and sits on the understander's feet as if on a stool. The feet are then extended up and back (photo 5.24). The physics is very simple: The understander supports the weight of the top-mounter plus that of his own legs. If that person is about the same weight, all that is added is the weight of the legs. It is almost as if the legs are attached upside-down to the other person. The top person does not have to do much of anything if the bottom person knows how to balance her, and if the bottom person does not now how to balance her, there is little she can do anyway. For greater safety, you should use a mechanic (chapter eight), or at least one spotter. There are other possibilities with inverted columns, including balancing two-high, feet-to-feet (photo 5.25).

You can also support a top-mounter by holding her feet in your hands. It is best to learn this trick with the understander on his back so that the top-mounter is not too far off

PHOTO 5 24

PHOTO 5.25

PHOTO 5.26a

PHOTO 5.26b

the ground. The understander lies on the floor with his hands in a palms-up position beside his shoulders. The top-mounter stands on the hands and the understander grips her feet. The top-mounter then jumps up while the understander thrusts his arms straight up. It may be helpful to do this with a mechanic at first. It is very important for the top-mounter's feet to be as pointed as possible. Her knees should be locked, her body straight and her arms at her sides or behind her back. The understander does the balancing. It is somewhat like balancing a cue stick: It is harder than balancing one but easier than two. In a good feet-to-hands, the understander can bring the top-mounter's feet together. He should not let them get any wider than shoulder distance.

To press the top-mounter up, the understander lies on his back with his forearms at his sides in a vertical position. He raises one leg for the top-mounter to hold while she steps into his hands with her feet pointed (photo 5.26a). The top-mounter then releases the understander's leg and he presses her up until his arms are fully extended (photo 5.26b).

The two-high. feet-to-shoulders can serve practical purposes as well, such as having the top-mounter rig a trapeze (photo 5.27). In his film, *Neighbors* (Metro Pictures Corporation, 1920), Buster Keaton finds a practical use for a three-high, feet-to-shoulders. Keaton wants to elope with the girl next door, but her father disapproves of the match and locks her upstairs. Keaton takes two accomplices into his house. Soon afterwards, the "understander" steps out of the bottom window and a "middleman" steps out of a second floor

PHOTO 5.27

window onto his shoulders. Keaton then steps out of the third story onto his shoulders. Three-high, they start to walk over to the girl's house, but suddenly the girl's father comes out and so they run back and retreat into their windows. When the coast is clear, they cautiously come out again and cross over to her house. Keaton takes her out through the third-story window and three-high (four in all), they make their getaway down the street. They come to a scaffolding and Keaton jumps off the shoulders of the middleman and carries the girl across the top level while the middleman runs across the lower level and the understander runs underneath. At the end of the scaffolding, they jump back into the three-high. Suddenly the middleman gets swept off by a line stretched across their path, but Keaton and his fiancée land on the shoulders of the understander, who keeps on running as though nothing had ever happened. A few seconds later, the understander falls into an open cellar, but Keaton manages to step off his shoulders just in time to keep going, his bride-to-be still in his arms.

6

Tumble vaulting

In tumble vaulting, the performer executes partial, full or multiple rotations of the body around any of its three basic axes in either of two alternate directions. In doing this, the body may be required to assume specific attitudes which presuppose a high degree of flexibility, particularly of the hips, spine and shoulders. Definitions of tumbling, acrobatics and contortion vary, but tumble vaulting certainly includes elements of all three.

The body has a long axis that goes from top to bottom, a medium axis from left to right and a short axis front to back. You do not always turn exactly around one of these axes, and you may turn on more than one at once. You can rotate in two possible directions around any axis. My students begin tumble vaulting by doing a pirouette (long axis) left and right, a roll (medium axis) forward and backward and a cartwheel (short axis) left and right. This familiarizes them with the basic axes and directions.

Pirouette

If you jump up into the air vertically and turn a few degrees to the left or right so that the body rotates around its head-to-feet axis, you have begun to learn the pirouette. By increasing the amount of turn, you can execute a quarter, half, one-and-a-half, double or even triple pirouette. The full single pirouette is a 360° turn on the long axis of the body (photos 6.1a-e). Pulling the arms in close to the body will help to accelerate the turn. Pirouetting in one direction may seem easier than in the other direction, but by learning both you can expand your range of movement.

PHOTO 6.1b

PHOTO 6.1b

PHOTO 6.1c

PHOTO 6.1d

PHOTO 6.1e

The pirouette is very much a part of dance and bullfighting. When combined with other tumble vaulting tricks, it is usually called a twist. If it is performed continuously in a point of suspension (chapter eight) or on a point of support (chapter five), it might also be called a spin.

Forward roll

On the medium (left to right) axis, the basic exercise is the forward roll. There are many different variations, but the most basic is a tucked roll executed with the body tucked in a ball-like position. You can warm up for the forward roll by grabbing your knees and rocking back and forth along your back. This will give you the feeling of rounding your back and keeping your chin to your chest.

To do a forward roll, squat down and place your hands on the mat near your knees but not too far out in front of you (photo 6.2a). The knees, feet and arms should stay shoulder-width apart and your chin should be tucked to your chest. The top of your head does not come in contact with the floor. As the back of your head gently touches the floor, round your back, tuck into a ball, keep your knees to your chest and push off with your feet (photo 6.2b). Push the floor with your hands as you roll until your legs are over your head (photo 6.2c). As you roll onto your back, do not flatten out or throw your head back, but instead stay rounded with the chin tucked to the chest (photo 6.2d). Continue rolling straight ahead and bring your feet in closer and closer to your hips (photo 6.2e) until they touch the floor (photo 6.2f). To stand

PHOTO 6.2a

PHOTO 6.2c

PHOTO 6.2b

PHOTO 6.2d

PHOTO 6.2e

PHOTO 6.2f

PHOTO 6.2g

up, reach forward with the arms and shoulders, and look straight ahead (photo 6.2g). Sometimes women come out of the roll with knees together and feet wide, whereas men will do the opposite and come up with the knees apart and the feet together. A more neutral solution is to keep the knees and ankles shoulder-distance apart. It is important to do the forward roll well because it is at the base of many of the more advanced exercises in tumble vaulting.

Cartwheel

The third basic exercise is the cartwheel, in which you turn along the short (front to back) axis. To warm up, it is a good idea to do several right and left kicks to each side to about waist level.

To do a cartwheel to the left, stand straight with your left arm raised, right arm to the side and feet apart along an imaginary straight line. Turn the head to the left and look at the spot on the floor where the left arm will be placed (photo 6.3a). Bend the left knee a little and place your left hand along that same imaginary line. The right arm touches the floor shoulder distance from the left arm, again along the same imaginary line (photo 6.3b). Kick the right leg up briskly as you straighten the left leg. Make sure you put your hands down flat on the floor for the best support of your weight. The eyes remain focused between your hands. The combined kicks of the left and right legs should bring you through a straddle handstand position (photo 6.3c). Keep the legs wide apart and straight with the toes pointed and stretch upward through the

shoulders and torso. As the left arm leaves the floor, the right leg will land on the floor (photo 6.3d). Push off with the right hand and stretch up toward the ceiling as the left leg lands, bringing you to a standing position (photo 6.3e).

The cartwheel is done in one continuous, smooth and rhythmic movement. The elbows and knees are kept as straight as possible. In the beginning, you may not wish to kick all the way up to the vertical position. You can practice by starting with low kicks that are somewhat less than vertical. As you feel more confident, kick higher and straighter. Even if the kick is small, try to do the cartwheel in a straight line. If your arms or legs are not in a straight line, you may lose your balance and end up sitting on the floor. Since the cartwheel passes through a handstand position (chapter two), any work done on the handstand can help improve your cartwheel. Learn the cartwheel to the right as well as to the left.

Basic principles

The pirouette, forward roll and cartwheel are the basis for all advanced tumbling techniques. Once you understand that there are three basic axes that you can turn on, and that you can turn in either direction, you can begin to explore the other possibilities. A qualified instructor can be helpful because you cannot see what your body is doing.

Your body can also be in different positions when it is turning: straight, tucked or arched. Another distinction can be made between ground, semi-aerial and aerial techniques. The terms ground and aerial are also

PHOTO 6.3a

PHOTO 6.3b

PHOTO 6.3c

PHOTO 6.3e

PHOTO 6.3d

used in the circus to distinguish between an act performed on the ground and an act performed high in the air, but that is not what is meant here. The forward roll is a good example of a ground technique because the body is rolling along the ground with no attempt to lift it into the air. The turn on the axis is taking place while you are on the ground. In a semi-aerial trick, your support goes from your feet to your hands to your feet. The cartwheel is therefore a semi-aerial trick, as are handsprings, round offs and walkovers. In an aerial trick, the body leaves the ground, turns no less than one complete rotation and then lands without the intermediate step. The pirouette is actually a very simple and safe example of an aerial technique, but aerial tricks on the other two axes are far more dangerous and difficult (aerial somersaults, aerial cartwheels, etc.). Although aerial tricks are usually more dangerous than semi-aerial tricks, they are not necessarily harder to learn. There are, for example, many people who can do an aerial back somersault but cannot do a flip-flop (back handspring).

You can also relate to space in different ways when you are tumbling. The most common patterns are in a straight line, in a circle or in place. Tumbling is usually done in a straight line down a mat, but tumbling in a circle is perhaps more relevant to the circus. Arab tumblers, for example, traditionally do tricks around the circumference of the ring.

Circular tumbling will of course affect your technique. If you are doing a cartwheel facing into the circle, you have to lean in. If you are facing out of the circle, you will have to lean back. When you do tricks in place on the

mat, you may well be exhibiting greater
control than if you did them moving through
space. Walkovers and back handsprings in
place are usually associated with a high degree of flexibility.

Aikido roll

The aikido roll, or shoulder roll, is taken from
the Japanese martial art of aikido. In executing it, you are turning around all three axes of
the body—long, medium and short.

Begin by placing your left foot forward and
holding your left wrist with your right hand so
that your arms form a hoop. Bend the left
knee until the knuckles of the right hand
come into contact with the mat (photo 6.4a).
The head turns to the right and does not
touch the mat during the roll. Continue rolling
diagonally along the left forearm (photo
6.4b), the left upper arm (photo 6.4c) and
across the left shoulder (photo 6.4d). Continue down along the back, from the upper
left to the lower right (photo 6.4e). Bend your
right knee so that the left leg is crossed over
it (photo 6.4f). Step over your right calf with
your left foot, placing it on the mat (photo
6.4g). As you stand up, turn to face the direction from which you came (photo 6.4h).

You can do the roll slowly and check yourself to see if you are doing each step correctly. The pattern is a straight line on the
floor which your body crosses diagonally.
Very often a student will do a good aikido roll
but find himself rolling off the mat because he
did not match the line of his roll with the
center line of the mat. Be sure to learn the

PHOTO 6.4a

PHOTO 6.4c

PHOTO 6.4b

PHOTO 6.4d

94 Circus techniques

PHOTO 6.4e

PHOTO 6.4f

PHOTO 6.4g

PHOTO 6.4h

aikido roll to the right as well as to the left.

Variations on rolls

To execute a symmetrical backward roll, squat down with the feet and knees shoulder-distance apart. Tuck your chin to your chest and keep it tucked during the entire roll. Push off and roll back staying tucked in a ball. When you start to roll over your upper back and shoulders, place your hands on each side of your head with the fingers pointing toward the shoulders and push until you are on your feet again. When rolling, the knees and feet stay shoulder-distance apart on each side of the head. Stay tucked, keep chin tucked to chest throughout, keep your eyes open and do your roll in one continuous movement. Some students turn the head to the side instead of keeping it straight so that they do not actually roll over the head.

There is also an asymmetrical backward shoulder roll which is almost an aikido roll in reverse. Sit down with one knee straight and the other bent. If the left leg is bent, push off with the left foot, roll back and turn your head to the right side. As you roll over your right shoulder, bring the right knee to the mat in front of your face. Straighten the left leg and swing it over and backward. You will end up kneeling on your right knee. Bring the left leg forward, place the left foot on the floor and stand up.

This back roll is very commonly used by jugglers, particularly the Chinese, because it leaves the hands free. It is especially useful if you are spinning a plate in either or both hands. If you are going to roll over your right shoulder, it will be easier to hold something in your left hand because it will be higher and therefore you can see it. Of course you could be spinning plates in both hands at the same time.

Buster Keaton used this roll very effectively in *College* (United Artists, 1927), where he plays a student working as a waiter. He is carrying soup from the kitchen when he drops a napkin from his arm. He turns around to pick it up and gets knocked over backwards by another waiter coming out of the kitchen. Keaton then executes this back shoulder roll from a standing position without spilling the soup.

Forward and backward rolls can also be done with the legs straight, either together or out to the side in a straddle. There is also a whole series of forward and backward rolls without hands. Other good variations include doing a forward roll from a headstand or a handstand (chapter two). When doing it from a handstand, be sure you are overbalanced forward before you tuck into the roll. You can also do front and back rolls into headstands and handstands.

Tiger leap

The tiger leap (dive roll) is a diving forward roll. The main difference between it and the forward roll is that in the tiger leap your feet leave the mat *before* your hands hit the mat. Start in a squat position, as if you are going to do a forward roll. Stretch your arms forward keeping your head between them. Look straight ahead. Push off with your feet,

straighten your legs and reach out, placing your hands further forward than you would for a forward roll. Then try this from a standing position.

Eventually you may be able to do this from a run with a take-off from both feet (photo 6.5). It is possible to leap through a hoop (photo 6.6), over a chair (photo 6.7), or between the legs of someone doing a straddle headstand (photo 6.8).

The most critical aspect of the tiger leap is the landing. The body descends to the floor at approximately a 45° angle. First the palms of the hands hit the floor and the arms "plié" (photo 6.9a) with the same kind of resistance that the legs offer when you land on your feet. Then the head is tucked (photo 6.9b) and immediately thereafter the upper back is rounded (photo 6.9c). Continue the roll up onto your feet.

Buster Keaton used tiger leaps throughout his movies. He does a whole series of them in *The Scarecrow* (Metro Pictures Corporation, 1920) in a scene where a dog is chasing him. In *Sherlock Jr.* (Metro Pictures Corporation, 1924), he escapes through a window and at the same time dives into a woman's costume that he had placed in the opening beforehand. When the villains come after him, all they find is a little old lady. My favorite is in *The Goat* (Metro Pictures Corporation, 1921) where Keaton manages to escape from a locked room by going from the seat of a chair, to a table, to the shoulders of his would-be assailant (Joe Roberts) and from there he does a tiger leap through the transom above the locked door.

PHOTO 6.5

PHOTO 6.6

PHOTO 6.7

PHOTO 6.9a

PHOTO 6.9c

PHOTO 6.8

PHOTO 6.9b

One-arm cartwheel

A good advanced variation on the cartwheel is the one-arm cartwheel. It is actually not too different. You do not really need the second hand because if you do a right-sided cartwheel correctly, your left foot is going to come down next to your left hand, which means your left hand is somewhat superfluous. If you concentrate on kicking and getting over, you should be able to get your left foot close enough. You can always have your other hand ready to put down if need be.

People assume that there is going to be a lot of weight on the right hand. However, if you kick with enough strength and speed to get the hips over, there is absolutely no such problem. Those who can do a regular cartwheel should be able to do a one-arm cartwheel. It is timing, not strength, which makes it possible. In fact, you should probably go to work on it right away so that you do not become afraid of it. The one-arm cartwheel can be done on either the first hand that comes around or the second. If you are doing it to the right, you do not have to do it with the right arm: You could also do it on the left arm.

Round off

Before executing a round off, first learn to do a running cartwheel. Take a short run, hop on the left foot, step down on the right foot and do a good cartwheel. The cartwheel will be faster because of the run, but otherwise the form remains the same. The hop and step

is called a hurdle. As you go into the hurdle, lean forward into your cartwheel. You should find you get over with ease using the run and hurdle.

Once you can do a running cartwheel, you can begin to learn the round off. The basic purpose of the round off is to convert forward momentum into backward momentum. If your cartwheel is very straight, you will have a better chance of doing a good round off.

Start by again taking a short run and going into a hurdle. Begin to do a right-sided cartwheel, but just as the legs are up and over the head, snap the legs and feet together as you twist the hips to precisely a one-quarter turn to the right. Push off with both hands at once, stretching through the shoulders and snap the feet down to the mat, bending the knees somewhat. You should be standing up straight with your arms up facing exactly the opposite direction from the way you began the trick.

Tumbling and flexibility

Pirouettes, forward rolls and cartwheels do not require a great deal of flexibility. However, many of the advanced tricks do depend on a good backbend and/or split. This is true of walkovers, limbers, aerial cartwheels, handsprings and many other techniques. For these, the student is well advised to work on developing the necessary flexibility before attempting to learn them.

The first exercise for your back is to push up into a backbend from the floor. Lie on your back with your knees up, your heels on the floor, your hands flat on the floor behind

your shoulders and your fingers pointing towards your feet. You then push up into an arched position (photo 6.10), which is sometimes called the "bridge." Your heels should remain on the floor and you will be looking between your hands. You can gradually work on bringing your feet closer to your hands and your shoulders directly over your hands, but at first you should be satisfied with whatever stretch you can achieve without straining. You can make the bridge harder by taking away one arm or leg. Kicks in this position are called "pony kicks." You could walk forward, backwards or to either side, and this is known as the "crab walk."

The most important backbend variation is the inside-out. It is easier to learn this against a wall or stall bars, and then work your way down to the floor. Stand with your legs straight and your arms straight against the wall as you lean on it from a distance of about three feet (91.44 cm). Your palms remain up for the entire trick and your feet travel along a line parallel to the wall. You begin by twisting your hips to the right and bringing the left foot around to the right. Then you bring your left hand around to the right until it is against the wall with the palm up. Your right hand comes around next and is placed against the wall with the palm up. Finally, the right foot swings around into place. You should be looking at your hands throughout the whole trick or you will not be able to bend properly. If you are doing it on the stall bars or against a wall, you should do it lower and lower until eventually you are doing it on the floor. On the floor, your foot leads as you go into it and your hand leads

PHOTO 6.10

as you come out of it. The inside-out is a very good exercise because it gives your hips the strength to hold your body up in a backbend.

In a backbend and up, you go from a standing position into a backbend on the floor and then rock back up into a standing position. You can utilize stall bars for this if you have them. Start in a standing position with your arms stretched over your head. It may be easier to go up on the toes, but you are not getting the full stretch, so keep your feet flat on the floor. Beginning the stretch in the upper back, lean back as far as you can go without bending your knees. When you cannot go any further, start to bend your knees a little bit, but at the same time be sure to keep your hips forward and toward the ceiling. Your head is bent back and your eyes are constantly looking for the floor. Go over as slowly as possible, and as soon as your hands hit you must make sure that you are in a tight backbend. In order to come up, first rock horizontally from the shoulders to the hips. Push up when the knees are as far over the feet as possible. Reach up with your arms: Do not let them fall to your sides.

With a good backbend, a good split, a good handstand and a good instructor, you are ready to work on highly advanced tumbling skills. It is very difficult to teach yourself advanced tumbling and acrobatics but—unlike most of the other chapters in this book—there is no dearth of excellent teachers and books. The treatment of tumbling in *Tumbling Techniques Illustrated* by Ted Burns (New York: A. S. Barnes, 1957) and *Tumbling Illustrated* by L. L. McClow (New York: A. S. Barnes, 1930) is quite systematic.

Once you can do a backbend and up, the first progression is to the front over, or front limber, in which you go into a momentary handstand, down into a backbend and then back up to a standing position. If you do this one leg at a time, with the legs in a stride split, you are doing a walkover. Walkovers can be done both forward and backward and even without the hands (aerial walkovers). The front handspring is a running trick, but it is very similar to the front limber because you are using a backbend and arch: Kick up and through the handstand position, arching the back and landing on your feet. The flip-flop, or back handspring, is used to build up backward speed that can be converted into upward speed; it is often done out of a round off, sometimes as a preparation for a back somersault. The body is thrown up and back, the hands hit the floor with your body in a handstand position and you snap down into a standing position. Again you should be able to do a backbend and up before you attempt the flip-flop, for then you will have sufficient flexibility, as well as the experience of going backwards.

Aerial tricks include aerial cartwheels and aerial somersaults. The aerial cartwheel is a running cartwheel without hands and is essentially a matter of running fast, doing a strong hurdle and kicking hard enough. They are easiest for people with a good straddle split, but can also be done through speed. There is also something called a brandy (or borani), which is basically an aerial round off. Buster Keaton did a brandy in *The Three Ages* (Metro Pictures Corporation, 1923): He is playing football and, as he is about to be tackled, he does a brandy right over the football.

An aerial front somersault is much more difficult than a back because you cannot see the floor until it is all over. You jump up, drive your hips toward the ceiling, tuck and then come out of it when you are three-fourths of the way through the turn. The aerial back somersault can be done standing or out of a round off or flip-flop. You do a backward layout jump, but instead of continuing with the arch, you tuck, bring your knees to your chest and land on your feet. Keaton does a standing back somersault in *Coney Island* (Paramount Famous Players-Lasky, 1917).

I feel it was no accident that Keaton was both an excellent acrobat and a master of the comic pratfall, but he recognized an important distinction between the two:

One reason Sennett did not hire trained acrobats for his Keystone force was because a trained acrobat seldom can get laughs in pictures when taking a comedy fall. He looks what he is, a trained acrobat doing his stuff, instead of a character in the picture taking a tumble accidentally. The only trained acrobat I ever saw who would take a fall and make it look funny was Poodles Hanneford, the great circus clown.

Though I have been called an acrobat I would say I am only a half-acrobat, at most. I did learn to fall as a kid, just as Chaplin, Lloyd and Fairbanks did. And I taught myself a few acrobatic tricks, including the round-off back somersault and other simple stunts. I could do butterflies, a series of cartwheels in a circle, without touching hands to the floor. But anyone who ever saw me throw a flip-flap realized I wasn't a professional acrobat. Audiences think a back somersault, in which you regain your feet without touching the floor, is dif-

PHOTO 6.11a

PHOTO 6.11c

PHOTO 6.11b

PHOTO 6.11d

ficult. But much more difficult to do is the flip-flap, a back somersault in which your hands do touch the floor. The back somersault only looks harder. What I do know about is body control.*

Tumble vaulting requires, and at the same time develops, the ability to fall without injuring yourself. If you do study tumbling, you will be hitting the ground in a variety of positions and you will intuitively learn how to avoid getting hurt. And since you could easily fall while practicing any of the activities in this book, some tumbling work could prove most valuable.

In breaking a fall, the objective is always to spread the impact out over as large an area and over as long a period of time as possible. Anything that makes the impact less direct, such as mats that give as you hit, is helpful. If you can roll out of a fall, the impact will be spread out over your whole body and delayed in time as if it were happening in slow motion. There should be relaxation, but this is not foolproof. If your muscles are too relaxed, you might break your bones. If you are not relaxed enough, you may bruise muscles. It is therefore a matter of being somewhat tense and then relaxing as you hit so that the impact is sustained by the muscles before the bones.

Whenever you are landing on your feet, you should plié as much as is necessary. You absorb the shock by bending the knees upon impact. You must bend your knees to jump up off the ground, so be sure to bend them an equal amount on landing. This is one rea-

son why the use of catapults (chapter nine) can be so dangerous: You may be thrown into the air with more power than your legs could supply and then land with a force that no plié can counteract.

Theatrically, falls and certain rolls have always been used for their effectiveness in performance. They played an important part in the commedia dell'arte, particularly in the character of Arlecchino, and were also used extensively in the battle scenes in the Peking Opera. Even in the modern Chinese ballet *Red Detachment of Women* (1964), the villains did incredible falls. Buster Keaton used falls and tumbling throughout all of his early movies. One classic fall he did consisted of placing one leg up on a table (photo 6.11a and b) as if to tie his shoe and then putting the other leg up alongside it (photo 6.11c and d). It is something of a back roll with the hands slapping the mat, but it is very dangerous. Keaton performed it on television at a fairly old age; it is something one learns over a long period of time. I began learning it in 1961, but I never showed it to anyone until after Keaton's death in 1966.

*Buster Keaton. *My Wonderful World of Slapstick* (Garden City. New York: Doubleday 1960) p. 49.

Part three

Infinite possibilities

In gyroscopic juggling, the performer spins, twirls, swings or otherwise rotates and manipulates an inanimate object. "Gyroscopic" is taken from the word "gyroscope." The gyroscope is a simple scientific invention: a wheel mounted in a ring so that its axis is free to turn in any direction. When the wheel is spun rapidly, it will keep its original plane of rotation no matter which way the ring is turned. This tendency of a spinning body to resist any change in its rotation not only makes gyroscopic juggling possible, but it has also become an important part of navigation. Gyroscopic compasses are used to steer ships and airplanes, and gyrostabilizers (a gyroscope in a vertical plane) are used as a stabilizing device in ships and planes because they serve to oppose sideways motion. In gyroscopic juggling, the object being manipulated remains stable in a precarious balance position precisely because it is spinning. It is the gyroscopic motion that creates the stability, and the greater the spin in terms of r.p.m.'s (revolutions per minute), the more stable it will become.

In his book, *Gravity* (Garden City, New York: Doubleday, 1962), George Gamow gives some indication of the baffling qualities of gyroscopes:

Probably the most amusing application of the gyroscope was made by a French physicist, Jean Perrin, who packed a running aviation-gyro into a suitcase and checked it at the Paris railroad station. When the French equivalent of a redcap picked up the suitcase and, walking through the station, tried to turn a corner, the suitcase he carried refused to go along. When the astonished redcap applied force, the suitcase turned on its handle at an unexpected angle, twisting the red-

7

Gyroscopic juggling

cap's wrist. Shouting in French, "The Devil himself must be inside!" the redcap dropped the suitcase and ran away.

Those readers interested in the scientific principles of spinning might enjoy the above book, as well as John Perry's *Spinning Tops and Gyroscopic Motion* (New York: Dover, 1957).

A top is a good example of a gyroscope, but many of our examples are less pure. The devil sticks, for example, are stabilized by their gyroscopic motion without ever having to complete a full rotation. Like a pendulum, they are gyroscopic to a certain degree. In fact, a gyroscope can be viewed as a pendulum that goes over the top. It has an inertia of motion that partially overcomes the friction.

Gyroscopic juggling can be very popular with audiences. They rarely realize that it is all based on simple scientific principles. The greatest difficulty for the performer is in getting it started. It is quite easy, for example, to keep a rope spinning once it is going around. The major drawback of gyroscopic juggling is that it does require special equipment. You will, for example, find it considerably more difficult to spin just any old ball or plate. As is also the case in chapters eight and nine, the "infinite possibilities" are based on obtaining highly diversified and specialized equipment.

At the same time, spinning has a certain inevitability to it. If you take a policeman with a nightstick and put him on a street corner with nothing else in his hand, he is going to learn to twirl it—and it is not easy. It is definitely a folk pastime. Children have always played with spinning tops, as well as with hula-hoops and the more modern gyroscopic toys. Spinning is very basic and very international.

Devil sticks

The devil sticks are the most symmetrical form of gyroscopic juggling that I teach my students. The devil stick "defies gravity" as it is hit back and forth by two smaller handsticks. The larger stick is tapered so that it has a smaller diameter in the middle. As it approaches a horizontal position, it is struck near its end so that it spins around almost 180° (photo 7.1a); it is then returned (photo 7.1b) a similar number of degrees (photo 7.1c) by the other handstick. It will therefore be making a series of half-spins around its center of gravity while the stick remains more or less in a vertical plane in front of you.

There is nothing more basic and harmonious than using both hands symmetrically, and that is reason enough to begin gyroscopic juggling with the devil sticks: It is the only activity in this chapter where both hands do exactly the same thing. But although devil sticks are the most symmetrical, they are not really the purest gyroscopes. Strictly speaking, devil sticks may be more the equivalent of a pendulum than of a gyroscope. With a pure gyroscope, such as a spinning plate, the spin is in a single direction, and not in alternating two directions back and forth. However, instead of spinning all the way around, as would a true gyroscope, the devil stick is hit 180° to the right and then 180° back to the left, etc. On the other hand, it is spinning

PHOTO 7.1a

PHOTO 7.1b

PHOTO 7.1c

around its center and, like a gyroscope, it does gain stability as the speed increases.

I have also found that practice with the devil sticks can result in a noticeable improvement in one's toss juggling. Your hands are moving in opposition and you cannot force the rhythm as in toss juggling. You have to wait until the devil stick is in the right place and then hit it. As a result of having worked with the devil stick, many of my students have gained a much better sense of timing as it applies to toss juggling.

It is significant that the devil stick is tapered in toward the middle from both ends. When you hit it with the right handstick, you are hitting it up and to the left, and when you hit it with the left handstick, you are hitting it up and to the right. The left and right cancel each other out and as a result you are hitting it up. When the upward force of your hits is equal to the downward pull of gravity, the stick appears to float, which may be why it is called a devil stick: It defies natural law.

In order to maintain good control, you need to lay the devil stick over on each hit so that it is almost horizontal. You hit it near the top of the stick, sending it way over so that it is almost horizontal on the other side. A common error is to keep hitting it back and forth in a vertical position. This is most often done by people who view themselves as beginners, but the opposite should be the case: It is even more necessary for beginners to lay it all the way over.

You can start in a number of ways. One method is to place the devil stick vertically on the floor and then lay it way over to the right so that it is supported with the right handstick just a few inches off the floor. You then hit it with the right handstick up and over to the left handstick and continue from there. You might also start with it off the ground. Hold it in a horizontal position in front of you, using the handsticks to support it on each end. You then hit it over with one handstick while you quickly get the other one in position to hit it back.

You should make contact with the devil stick near its end. Although you use a hitting motion, it is not a strong striking motion. It is more like catching the devil stick on the handstick and pushing it over. If you do it with too much force you will break the sticks.

The basic idea is to get control of the devil stick as it goes back and forth, and this takes practice. If you hit the stick in the right place without hitting it too hard, and if you wait until it is in the right position, you will probably be able to do it. But you must hit it in the right spot. One common mistake is to hit it perfectly, but then not go up with it as it rises, and as a result your next hit is in the middle. Another difficulty occurs if you go up with it as it gets higher and then end up going higher than you can comfortably reach. It is also important to pay attention to both sides. Sometimes beginners concentrate on laying it over into the correct position, but without realizing that they are only doing this on one side and are totally neglecting the opposite side. If you are laying it over 90° from the vertical axis on one side but only 3° on the other side, you might as well be laying it over 3° on both sides. Naturally this will not keep it going. It has to be equalized on both sides, just like the rola-bola (chapter five).

The basic technique is not too difficult, although it may take time to get it going. It is certainly quite accessible to someone who has already worked with balance and toss juggling. Once you have mastered this back and forth move, you can try more difficult variations. It is possible, for example, to control the devil stick with only one handstick. You hit it and then pull the stick back and around and hit it on the other side. You are doing exactly the same movements, but now you have to be fast enough to hit it over and then get your handstick over to the other side and hit it. Every other hit is then backhanded.

You could also put your hand under your leg, or even behind your back, and hit it. You can let it go end for end and then hit it, rather than just tapping the same end back and forth. The devil stick would then be turning nearly 360° between each hit. You can also do take-aways (chapter four) with devil sticks: All that is needed is an extra pair of handsticks. If I am hitting it first, I get my left handstick out of the way right after my left hit so that my partner can move into place while I am making my right hit. When my partner steps in, I have to be sure to hit it slightly farther than usual—but without breaking the rhythm—so that it reaches him. My partner makes a left-handed hit and continues to control it until I step in and take it back. This is not particularly difficult as long as the two people can both do devil sticks and can agree on when the transfer will take place.

Although devil sticks have been known in the West for a long time, they originated in China and even today's Chinese acrobat-jugglers excel at devil sticks, In the Shen-

yang Acrobatic Troupe, they combine devil sticks with tumble vaulting. One woman performer hit the stick up in the air, did an aerial walkover, and still managed to catch it and continue. For a take-away, two women did a side-by-side (chapter four) with devil sticks and then a third woman came between them and took it away. One of their hardest tricks was to have two sticks going back and forth in opposition at the same time. While one handstick was engaging one devil stick, the other handstick was hitting the other devil stick. As a closing trick, it is quite common to spin the devil stick around the center of a single handstick in a single direction; this move resembles baton twirling and is far more gyroscopic than the basic devil stick moves. It can be done by hitting the large stick below the center each time it comes around. However, these women actually spun one on each handstick, which I had never seen before.

It is also possible to do many of these same variations with a tennis racket (photo 7.2). Use the same type of handsticks you used for conventional devil sticks.

Diabolo

The diabolo is an ancient Chinese pastime that has been known in the West since at least 1812. It was very popular in Europe around the turn of the century and even threatened to overshadow lawn tennis. A book on the subject, *Diabolo, the Game and Its Tricks* by David P. Ward, appeared in 1908 but is now out of print. The diabolo consists of two cones that are joined at their

PHOTO 7.2

PHOTO 7.3

apexes and it is spun, thrown and caught by means of a string that is attached at the ends to separate handsticks.

You begin by placing the diabolo on the ground and standing opposite one end of it. Insert the string under the waist of the diabolo. Bring the right handstick down close to the floor and the left handstick way up in the air. Try to maintain a 90° angle between the two parts of the string. Do not let the string hang loosely because you will need some tension in the string in order to manipulate the diabolo. It is like a pulley and V-belt: If there is not enough tension, it will slip off.

When you are ready, lift the right handstick to a position above your right shoulder, which will in turn rotate the diabolo to a position close to your left hand. When this point is reached, the right handstick is dropped back down almost to its original position. The right handstick is then immediately lifted back up above your right shoulder and the cycle begins again. It is very important to get as much spin as possible with that first pull. You can keep adding spin, and the more you add the more it stabilizes, just like a gyroscope.

The basic objective is to get a rapid spin going. The right hand is doing the work (photo 7.3). The diabolo is not symmetrical like the devil stick: It does not spin first one way and then the other. Instead it grips going one way and then is allowed to slip back the other way, just like a yo-yo "sleeping." Each time you lift the string up, you should be adding more and more spin to it.

If the front end tips down, you can pull the right handstick back as you stroke and it will straighten up. If it tips back, pull the right

handstick forward as you stroke. If it goes to the right or left, all I can suggest is that you turn with it. You must, however, maintain the spin at all times, because that is what keeps it stabilized. If it is not spinning at all, it simply will not balance, because its center of gravity is slightly above the string. The more spin the better.

Once you can keep it going, there are many variations you can try. You can throw it up in the air and catch it. This throw is achieved by moving the hands up and slightly out. The diabolo must have a good spin going when it is thrown or it may turn over in the air. Do not try to catch it holding the string slack. Stretch the string over your head in a somewhat horizontal position and catch the diabolo near one end of the string. The moment it comes down, let the string give and resume spinning it. You can also jump rope (over the string) while the diabolo is in the air or pass the diabolo by tossing it up and having a partner catch it. If you throw it when the r.p.m.'s are very high, the diabolo will leave the string with far more force than if it were spinning slowly.

You can also do an interesting variation using your foot. Push down on the string with your foot and lift with the stick nearest the diabolo. The diabolo will jump over your foot and can be caught on the other part of the string.

A valuable experience would be to spin it in the other direction. One of my students learned to throw it up into the air, do a half-pirouette, and then catch it, which meant that he had to be able to spin it with the opposite hand. The temptation is to learn it only one way because there seem to be so few tricks requiring you to be able to do it both ways. For performance, ambidexterity might not be necessary, but from a physiological point of view it would be good.

Rope spinning

Rope spinning has been popularized by cowboy movies and television westerns, but it is also a very good example of gyroscopic juggling. It was apparently originated toward the end of the eighteenth century by the Mexican rancher Don Juan Chavéz and was brought to the United States by a trick roper by the name of Vincente Oropeza, who performed in Buffalo Bill's Wild West Show. Will Rogers was the most famous, and probably the best, American to perform rope spinning.

When a rope is spinning it is more gyroscopic than the devil sticks. Rope spinning is particularly interesting because it can be done in vertical or horizontal planes and it also introduces the important concept of quasi-rigidity. When a lariat is being spun, it behaves as though it were rigid, and not like the amorphous mass that it is. The gyroscopic motion imparted by your wrist causes the rope to assume a circular shape and spin around a newly formed center. The gyroscopic force takes over and can even counteract the force of gravity

The basic exercise in rope spinning is to keep a large horizontal loop spinning around your body. You are going to rope yourself, but instead of pulling the rope tight and hogtieing yourself, you want to let the rope spin around you. You might try roping a chair just

to get the feeling for that. To rope something, you hold on to the spoke with the noose in your fingertips. You then try to throw this circular loop over the chair.

Starting the horizontal loop can be tricky. The stem is held in your right hand between the thumb and index finger about thirty inches (76.2 cm) from the honda. The last three fingers hold the noose loosely. Whatever you do, do not let go of the stem. The left hand holds on to the stem and the noose, shoulder-distance from the right hand (photo 7.4a). The right hand should spiral up (photo 7.4b) in a smooth movement to a point right above your head. As soon as your hand is around far enough to drop the noose outside of your arm (photo 7.4c), let go of the noose with both hands in such a way that the loop does not fall on your shoulder. You are using centrifugal force to get it billowed out and going around your body. You are then raising your right hand in a circular motion up over your left shoulder, back around and to the right of your head, dropping the noose and then bringing your hand to the center and rotating your wrist. To keep it going (photos 7.4d-f) you have to let the rope rotate in your hand, which can mean a certain amount of slippage. If you just grip it tightly, it will be okay for a while, but then the rope will start kinking up. You will find it very easy to *keep* it going once you *get* it going, though. The noose can even droop somewhat out of its horizontal plane and still maintain its stability; and if it does droop, it can be brought back into position by a smooth acceleration of the spin.

It is more difficult to get a vertical loop going in front of you. Instead of having grav-

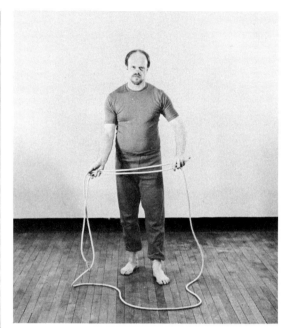

PHOTO 7.4a

PHOTO 7.4b

PHOTO 7.4c

PHOTO 7.4d

PHOTO 7.4e

PHOTO 7.4f

ity pulling down equally on the rope, as is the case with the horizontal loop, the honda is now rising up and around. The honda has to describe a vertical circle and pull the rope up with it. This is basically a matter of giving lift to it each time it comes around. It is lifted up and over the crest and then allowed to coast down, and then lifted up again, etc. It is difficult to get the vertical loop going because gravity tries to collapse the loop. Centrifugal force has to overcome gravity before the vertical loop can work.

Once you get the vertical loop going (photo 7.5), you can try something called the "Texas skip." It combines gyroscopic juggling with vertical vaulting in what may well be the greatest rope-jumping trick of all time. The rope-jumping part of it is the same as the rope-jumping in chapter three. You pull your knees up and jump through the loop as you pull the loop toward you. Once the rope reaches the end of its tether, you can pull back on it and jump back through the loop. There is an ideal moment for it to bounce back. If possible, see the Texas skip performed. It is a very rhythmic movement: over and back, over and back. You can create that rhythm yourself by taking the same amount of time on each side of the loop.

My students exhibit an unusual willingness to exert themselves with rope spinning until they master it. It can be very difficult to get the rope going that first time; it takes a lot of practice. But it is not too much of a strain, because you do not have to bend over and pick up the rope if you miss as you would with juggling balls or devil sticks. With each miss you can just stand there and pull the

PHOTO 7.5

loop back in, and try again. It is like having a built-in string attached to your prop. This can become a compulsion and, if you succeed, the compulsion deepens. This addiction is known as "roping fever."

It is of course difficult to put the technique for rope spinning into words so that the reader can just go out and do it. Nevertheless, there are a couple of good books on the subject that I do recommend: *Roping* by Bernard S. Mason (New York: A.S. Barnes, 1937) and *Will Rogers' Rope Tricks* by Frank Dean (Colorado Springs, Colorado: Western Horseman, 1969).

Foot juggling

You can also do gyroscopic juggling with your feet. This is known as foot juggling or "antipodism." It dates back at least to the Aztecs: When Cortéz conquered Mexico, he discovered a foot juggler and brought him back to Spain. In its simplest form you lie on your back with your legs perpendicular to the floor, balance a cylinder on one foot, and spin it around with the other foot. However, unless you are very flexible, it is a good idea to boost your hips up a little with a few pillows or a rolled-up mat. You could also use a cradle. This is a board supported at an angle of approximately 30° to the ground; it has two shoulder supports to keep you from sliding off. This will make it easier for you to engage your feet with the object you are foot juggling.

The first exercise is simply to toss the cylinder straight up and catch it on your feet. Toss the cylinder straight up on a vertical line, at the same time keeping your feet just

PHOTO 7.6

PHOTO 7.7

behind this line. Do not throw it much higher than the spot where your feet will be. If you bring your feet under it, you should be able to catch it. Your feet should be about shoulder-width apart and it will be easier if you really engage the arch of your foot. This position would be similar to standing on the inside edges of your feet instead of flat on your feet. Your heel and toe should be at the same height so that support is horizontal. This is achieved mostly with the ankles, but other artic-ulations are possible, such as with the knee. In the beginning, it is sufficient to just get the cylinder roughly centered with the feet shoulder-distance apart. A slightly more sophisticated method consists of bringing the supporting foot closer to the center of your body and the center of the cylinder more directly over this foot.

Once the cylinder is on your feet, you choose to either balance it on your left foot and spin it with your right foot (photo 7.6), or vice versa (photo 7.7). You are balancing the cylinder on one foot and kicking the end of it around at least 180° with the other foot. It is not a matter of hitting it with the front of your foot so much as it is of pedaling and pushing it around with the bottom of your foot (photos 7.8a-c). This is similar to riding a scooter, where you have one foot on the platform and the other pedaling against the ground. The cylinder stays up better if you spin it fast and it is actually fairly difficult to do it slowly: The greater the spin, the greater the stability.

It is important to remember that the weight of the cylinder remains essentially on one foot while the other foot is turning it. The other foot does not take the weight of it, it

PHOTO 7.8a

PHOTO 7.8c

PHOTO 7.8b

only pushes it around. If it does take the weight of the cylinder, it will tend to push it off the supporting foot. Sometimes people push it down under their heel. The cylinder has to stay over the heel without hooking under the toe.

It may not be necessary to hit the cylinder every time it comes around. The greater danger is that you will only turn it 90°, which leaves it in a difficult balance point. It is very easy for it to get stuck there. Turn it 180°. If it can coast another 180°, you need not kick it again. The pushing foot does follow through somewhat, and it can also "cheat" and reach back to join the cylinder a bit early.

It is possible to combine foot juggling with other skills, such as foot juggling while in a headstand or even a handstand. You can also foot juggle other kinds of objects. A simple, classic variation is to have the ends of the cylinder flaming. It is also possible to manipulate larger objects, such as tables and barrels. A barrel, for example, can be turned three ways: like a cylinder; as if you were walking under it, so that it rolls along the feet; or so that it turns over end for end along its vertical axis. Valentin Filatov of the Moscow Circus taught a bear to do it all three ways. Another standard prop is a "cross-pâté," sometimes referred to as a Maltese cross. (✚) There are several ways to spin it, but the most common is to step on each section of the cross so that it turns as your feet make a walking movement. Finally, foot juggling is often a part of flea circuses. The trained flea lies on its back and walks its feet under a tiny painted ball. For the flea, it is like a treadmill, but it looks like antipodism.

Spinning a plate on a stick

Spinning a plate on the end of a stick is similar to the horizontal loop we discussed in rope spinning. The plate is given a horizontal spin that goes in only one direction. To maintain this spin, the stick must describe a circle along the rim of the plate. The plate you use must have an uninterrupted circular rim, or you will have little chance of spinning it.

I introduce my students to plate spinning by using aluminum plates that have a good rim and taper to a point under the center. The first step is to place the center of the plate on the end of a pointed stick and then use your free hand to start the plate spinning in this position (photo 7.9). Unless you keep the spin going with your hand, it will eventually die out and the plate will fall off the stick. What you can do is to smoothly bring the point of the stick to the rim of the plate and describe a circle with the stick hugging the rim (photo 7.10). This will accelerate the spin and keep it going as long as you are making a circle with the stick. If you want, you can now bring the stick back to the center and let it coast for a while.

It is more difficult, but also more exciting to do this with an ordinary plate. However, if the plate does not have this indentation in the center, you can only use the rim to spin it. The classic approach is to take the stick in your hand, wind up and spin the plate outwards and then engage the rim with the stick and immediately begin describing a circle. I have also been able to get it going by adapting the method we used for the aluminum

plates. I put the center of the plate on top of the stick and give it a spin with my right hand, and then quickly get my right hand to the bottom of the stick by the time the end of the stick engages the rim of the plate.

If you spin the plate too slowly, it will droop or appear to wobble. As long as it has not yet fallen off, the speed of its spin will keep it going for a while. If you smoothly speed up the spin, you will regain the stability. It is important not to panic just because it is wobbling. A gyroscopic object's tendency to stay in place is incredible. Even if it is wobbling, you probably have plenty of time left. Normally the plate is in a horizontal position with a horizontal spin, but it can droop almost to a vertical position without completely losing its stability.

As is true of most gyroscopic juggling, all of your movements with the stick must be as smooth as possible. You cannot go fast and then go slow. You have to make a full circle with the stick so that you are always pushing out against the rim. You cannot cut across the circle or make a smaller circle than the diameter of the rim. In fact, you should actually make what feels like a slightly larger circle just to be sure.

Ball spinning

Jugglers who specialize in this are always looking for well-balanced balls that are suitable for spinning. Larger balls are generally easier to spin, and you can put patches on the ball and even sand the surface in an attempt to achieve the best distribution of weight. Sometimes it helps to have the ball

PHOTO 7.9

PHOTO 7.10

slightly deflated so, as with the aluminum plates, there is an indention for your finger. You should also determine the ball's center of gravity by putting it in water: the heaviest part will sink to the bottom. Mark the top and always keep that end up when you are spinning the ball, otherwise you will have something of a goof ball.

The trick to spinning a ball on your finger is about 99% getting it going after which point it is very easy. To catch it on your finger, throw the ball up, let your hand go up with it and then meet it on the way down; your hand should come down at almost the same speed as the ball. Do not put your elbow out to the side when you are throwing and catching the ball: It should be perpendicular to the floor and therefore right under the ball. The spin does not last forever. When the ball begins to wobble, you should have to catch it and start over again. Balls can be spun on mouthsticks and it is also common to place a small ball on top of a large ball and spin both of them at the same time. Francis Brunn does an incredible trick with two balls. He spins a large ball on his finger and lets a small ball roll from a balance on his forehead to a balance on the nape of his neck, and lets it drop behind him, kicking it up with the back of his heel so that it lands on top of the spinning ball and the two of them spin together.

Baton twirling

This has generally been used by women and limited to a certain musical function, particu- larly as part of a marching band, but some jugglers have taken an interest in it. Norman Crider won an international juggling competi- tion (the Rastelli festival) as a baton twirler, although he doesn't consider himself a jug- gler. Baton twirling is actually an American adaptation of Swiss flag manipulation. A Swiss flag troupe toured the United States and a cer- tain number of Americans learned to do it, eventually eliminating the flag and develop- ing the baton as a whole separate idea. The baton as we now know it is a slender metal rod with a ball at each end. Most baton moves are based on the rotation of the wrist, but there are some moves in which the baton is manipulated by the individual fingers. The basic variations include hand transfers, twirl- ing it around the body, tossing it into the air and catching it and shoulder, elbow and neck rolls. Some of these moves can and have been done with canes and tennis rac- kets. There are several books on baton twirl- ing. One of the most thorough is Constance Atwater's *Baton Twirling* (Rutland. Vermont: Charles E. Tuttle. 1964).

Weapons manipulation

It is common to see soldiers go through intri- cate drills in which they spin a weapon around its center as if it were a baton. In Chinese terms, it is this familiarity with the weapon that makes one good at using it. This would include rifle manipulation and gun spin- ning. as well as drawing and holstering a pistol. Of the countless varieties of Chinese spinning martial arts weapons, perhaps the most notable is the "devil's fork" or ringing trident, which is manipulated around the body as well as spun like a baton. Other examples of gyroscopic weapons manipulations include the Australian boomerang and the Argentinian bola. The boomerang is shaped like an air- plane wing: flat on the bottom and curved on the top. It is aerodynamic so that as it spins through the air, it will lift, sail out, and (if it does not hit its target) sail back into your hand. In its simplest form the bola consists of a rope with a weight on each end. It is thrown so that, as it engages its prey, it continues to loop around the animal.

Knife throwing

A certain amount of controlled spin is in- volved in knife throwing, as well as in throw- ing tomahawks, battleaxes, etc. Hunters usu- ally throw from the handle so they can keep the blade very sharp, whereas showmen pre- fer to hold the blade, in which case the knife will be making a turn and a half. The classic routine involves just missing a live target. In the early days of television they did a version of it in which the knife is thrown backwards as another knife pops out of the target.

Throwing plates

We know from toss juggling rings and plates that, as curvilinear objects, they tend to stabil- ize as a result of their gyroscopic motion. This same principle applies to the act in which a single person catches a large number of plates thrown by several other performers in a smooth rhythm. This was performed very well by Oskal-Ool in the Moscow Circus. He catches them at an incredible speed, turning them over and putting them on his other arm. By the end of the trick, the plates are coming at him only a few feet behind one another. No one person could throw them that fast, so it is essentially a matter of synchronizing the throws of several people.

Spinning top

The top is quite an ancient toy. Its social history is well documented in D. W. Gould's *The Top* (New York: Potter, 1973). The top is conical in shape and has a steel point on which it can be spun. The spin is usually imparted by unwinding a string that is wrapped around the top, but I have also seen a rubber band contraption that could shoot the top out like a gun as the rubber band unwound. I have only seen two circus performers do acts with tops. One performer made it climb up a string as if it were a diabolo, whereas the other top specialist spun it on various parts of his body.

Yo-yo

This common toy is an invention of the Philippines. It is highly concentric and highly gyroscopic. It is a thick, grooved double disk with a string attached to its center. The yo-yo is made to rise and fall to the hand by unwinding and rewinding this string. It is sometimes called a yo-yo top because it is like a top that does a vertical spin. Duncan is probably the largest manufacturer of yo-yos. They publish a booklet on the subject and also have their own yo-yo expert who demonstrates the more difficult tricks.

Meteor bowls

This consists of a rope with bowls of water in triple suspension. They are swung around both vertically and horizontally, but the centrifugal force holds the water in the bowls. In the film *Springtime in Kwangchow*, an acrobat doing this was able to keep the spin going while doing a back somersault off a partner's shoulders.

Parasol spinning

Another classic Chinese act is performed with a parasol and ring. I use a deck tennis ring or a ring about that size, but it can also be done with a ball. It is not particularly difficult. Put a reverse spin on the ring, throw it up and catch it on the parasol, and then twirl it with the stem of the parasol. It works like a gear because they are rolling together. You can tip it, move it, speed it up, slow it down, and it will more or less roll in place, although it can also travel around the circumference of a parasol.

Hoop rolling

This is another old pastime; children used to roll hoops as a game, striking the top of the hoop with a stick to steer it and keep it going. More advanced routines can be performed with wooden bicycle rims if you have a good wooden floor. Howard Nichols did a whole act in which he made the hoops take "edges" and follow arranged patterns. He set up a screen that formed a little coop and then

rolled a series of hoops so that each one went around in a diminishing spiral, finally falling inside the coop one after another. The last one always missed, went around a second time, and then went in. It takes unbelievable practice and precision to give those hoops the right amount of speed and angle. It is also possible to give them "English," a reverse spin that makes them slide across the floor like a yo-yo that is sleeping and then roll back. You can also do this to a ball when you are toss juggling. If you give it a reverse spin and let it fall behind you, it will travel back to you.

Antithesis: eccentric spin

If I take my shoe and spin it around on a stick so the stick stays at a fixed point in the heel of the shoe, the spin would be basically eccentric. In other words, the pivot point is nowhere near the center of the shoe. All of our previous examples were concentric: the object was spinning around its center. This was even true of spinning a plate on a stick. Although the stick stayed on the rim, the plate was actually spinning around its own center.

The manipulation of flags, police nightsticks and Indian clubs all fall into the eccentric category because, unlike the baton, they are swung from one end of the object. The hula-hoop (U.S. patent no. 3,079,728), which was a very popular fad for a while, is also eccentric because it is spinning around its edge. This has its equivalent in the circus in the form of spinning rings around various parts of the body. You can take a single ring

and spin it eccentrically on your arm very
easily with an up and down movement of the
arm (photo 7.11). It is a little more difficult to
add another in the opposite direction (photo
7.12). This can be made increasingly more
complicated (photo 7.13).

The eccentric spin is also used in a trick
done with a pool rack, cue stick and glass of
water. The glass of water is placed down inside the rack and the cue stick is inserted
under the top corner and then rotated in order
to spin the rack and glass. You can then go
from a vertical to a horizontal loop without
losing the water. Next try to slow down in
such a way that you maintain the centrifugal
force and return it to the original position. No
trickery is necessary, although I am sure
some people watching think the glass is
attached in some way.

PHOTO 7.11

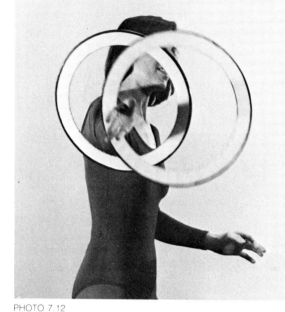

PHOTO 7.12

PHOTO 7.13

In rigging equilibristics, the performer directly or indirectly hangs from and/or balances upon aerial apparatus. This may consist of any traditional or original arrangement of such elements as rope, bars, rings, loops, pedestals, poles, etc., which are attached through suspension and/or compression to one or more anchoring points. Common examples include the trapeze, Roman rings, slack rope and tightrope. Certain pieces of rigging, particularly the trapeze, can also be used in catapult vaulting (chapter nine).

Because you are up in the air, rigging equilibristics may bring on the vertigo associated with fear of heights. If physically you are not up to something, you may feel dizzy. Part of this dizziness comes from the psychological awareness that you are physically unprepared for it. Height and motion can be dizzying, but as you grow more accustomed to it and feel less threatened by it, you experience less and less vertigo. That is how I got used to the trapeze: first by rigging it, then by sitting on it, and only then by doing it. Just because you get dizzy the first time does not mean you always will. You should proceed cautiously and just gradually develop the necessary confidence. If you are interested in psychological implications, you may find Michael Balint's theory of philobatism and ocnophilia, as expounded in his book *Thrills and Regressions* (New York: International Universities Press, 1959) as fascinating as I did.

If you are going to perform skills from this chapter, you will probably have to make a financial investment. You simply cannot fool with human life. You need equipment that is

8

Rigging equilibristics

absolutely safe, no matter what you have to pay for it. Do not use the wrong thing. Do not hang a trapeze with S-hooks. Most circus people are not daredevils and are very compulsive when it comes to safe rigging. Even so, when injury or death occurs, it is usually the rigging that has failed and not the performer.

It is not to be implied that you can somehow get away with using unsafe rigging because you are not a professional or if the rigging is only temporary. People have come to me and said: "I need a trapeze. Can't I just put little screw eyes in the ceiling and hang it from there?" I say no, you can't. "But it's only going to be for three seconds." Of course if it is going to be strong enough to hold for three seconds, it has to be strong enough to hold. And if it is strong enough to hold, it will certainly hold for three seconds. Let us not speak of things as "holding for a certain length of time before they collapse." People talk like that to me and it drives me nuts! Forget it!

Take advantage of the quality materials available, at least in the United States. Many pieces of rigging are purchased for one reason or another by the United States government, and therefore have to meet government specifications. This in effect dictates their strength and the alloys that go into them. Manufacturers do not make them below these standards, because then their largest customer would not be allowed to buy them. I have heard of people doing weird things, such as "testing" rigging by putting the pull of a tremendous weight on a shackle. If it holds, it passes the test, but of course the very testing of it is bound to cause metal stress which may lead to metal fatigue and result in a bad fall.

I generally divide rigging into "gymnastic" and "funambulistic." I use the term gymnastic to refer to those skills in which the body is suspended, often upside-down, by one or more of its extremities. In the animal world, the dormant state of bats is one of inverted prehension, which is to say they can do rigging equilibristics in their sleep. Funambulistics, which means rope walking, here refers to those activities in which the body is supported from beneath. These are not pure distinctions. Typically, the trapeze woud be gymnastic and the tightrope funambulistic, but it is possible to be supported from beneath by a trapeze or suspended from above by a tightrope.

Mechanic

A mechanic is a mechanical device for safety. It usually consists of a rope and pulley system hooked up to a safety belt worn by the performer. A spotter maintains some degree of control over the performer by holding on to the ropes (photo 8.1). It is one of the most basic examples of rigging, but it is a safety device and not a piece of performance rigging in the sense that the trapeze is.

The mechanic has traditionally been used in performance in Communist countries, but in the West it has mostly been used for training purposes. China's Shenyang Acrobatic Troupe uses a mechanic for dangerous tricks, and, as I've mentioned before, all students at the Moscow Circus School learn to spot with one. Nets are relatively strange and foreign to most of them, but they rarely do a perch pole or high wire act without a mechanic. It was not often seen in performance in the American circus until the Moscow Circus paid its first visit to the United States in 1963. It was felt that if you could not do a trick well enough to do it without a mechanic, then you simply did not do that trick in performance. Now it is quite commonly used in the United States, especially by acts from Eastern European countries. It does prevent accidents and makes it possible to attempt more difficult tricks.

The purpose of the mechanic is to insure the safety of the person you are spotting. If he gets into trouble, you use it to slow down the fall or to make sure that he lands right side up. If, however, you pull hard on the rope in order to keep him from coming down at all, you might injure his ribs. If there is not enough give, you could cause other injuries in the course of stopping the fall.

If the spotter is right-handed, he should wrap the rope around his left hand at least once before he grips it with that hand. If you do this, you might get pulled up into the air, but at least you will be counterbalancing the person you are spotting. If you do not do this, you may get a rope burn, let go of the rope, and allow the person to take a bad fall. It is common to wear a glove on the left hand while leaving the right hand ungloved. This further protects the left hand from rope burns and leaves the right hand free to manipulate the rope.

In addition to pulling the rope up and down, you can control it by walking back and forth or by taking the bite on your hand at different levels. Let us use spotting a two-high (chapter five) as an example. As the top-

PHOTO 8.1

mounter climbs up, the spotter can pull in a certain amount of rope. However, he should realize that the top-mounter may have to come down very quickly. It does not make sense to have all the slack out, reaching way up to grasp the rope. If he does come down, the spotter will get his hand squeezed and pulled and they may both end up dangling in the air. When the top-mounter goes up, the spotter walks backwards and brings the rope down. He can then walk forward and go back up again as the top-mounter comes down. The spotter might even be able to use the same grip but, in all likelihood, he will take a new bite when the top-mounter is in position. However, the spotter must be ready to grab the rope should the top-mounter start to lose balance while he is changing his grip. If the top-mounter is not centered under the mechanic, one rope may become too slack and the other too taut. It is the spotter's responsibility to make the necessary adjustments on the rope.

Trapeze

The trapeze in and of itself is simply a piece of rigging. It is usually used gymnastically. It can, however, be used funambulistically (balancing trapeze) or as a catapult (fly bar). The use of the fly bar for mounts, dismounts and swinging is discussed in chapter nine.

Hanging from the trapeze

The first thing we are going to do on the trapeze is a simple hang. You should already be warmed up and stretched out before you go up. Jump up and grab the trapeze with your hands shoulder-width apart, gripping the bar with your palms away from you. I strongly advise people to wrap their thumbs around the bar. Gripping the bar this way is much safer than just trying to hang from your fingers. There are exceptions: In a flying-return act, the leaper usually hangs without his thumbs gripping the fly bar so that his hands can slide on or off the bar with ease.

Once you are hanging on the trapeze, you should be as relaxed as possible except for those parts of the body involved in holding the bar. Do not pull on the bar; hang from it. In dropping off the trapeze, it is imperative to plié (bend your knees) as you hit so as to soften the fall. Do not land stiff-legged or with your knees already bent. This exercise acquaints the students with the trapeze and allows me to check how relaxed they are, whether they grip the bar properly, how they manage getting down and how well they follow instructions.

We next work on two basic exercises out of which almost everything else is developed: the bird's nest and the catcher's lock. The basic principles are the same in both, but their differences indicate the wide range of possibilities offered by the trapeze. If you learn how to do a bird's nest and a catcher's lock correctly, you will have a good foundation on which to build.

Bird's nest

The bird's nest is comparable to the bow pose (*dhanurasana*) in hatha yoga and promotes flexibility. Unlike its equivalent position on the ground, the only tension required is in your hands and feet. You are relaxing while gravity does the work, rather than using an effort and its attendant tensions to assume the position.

You jump up and grab the bar with your hands shoulder-distance apart and your thumbs wrapped around the bar (photo 8.2a). Looking straight ahead, you swing your legs back and forth from the hips. Swinging back from the hips with the knees bent is called the beat back (photo 8.2b). Swinging forward from the hips with the legs straight is called the beat forward (photo 8.2c). When you have built up enough momentum to get your legs to at least a horizontal position on the beat forward, contract the abdominal muscles, drawing your knees to your chest. This will get your feet right up to the bar between your hands. You need to work both feet under the bar (photo 8.2d) so that they are on the same side of the bar as your torso. To do so, you may have to begin by hooking just one toe on the bar and then working your way up and under. Some beginners even have to go diagonally in order to get through. You then flex your feet around the padded cables at the point where they meet the bar (photo 8.2e). Next slowly bring your pelvis right through your arms (photo 8.2f) and keep going until you are in an arched (bow) position with your arms bent behind you (photo 8.2g). Do not make any quick or violent movements: Just relax as much as possible.

To come down, return your pelvis to a "tuck" position, unhook your feet and use your stomach muscles to bring your legs down with control. The legs should come straight down. If you allow them to swing

PHOTO 8.2a

PHOTO 8 2d

PHOTO 8 2f

PHOTO 8 2b

PHOTO 8 2c

PHOTO 8 2e

PHOTO 8 2g

out in front, they create a momentum that could cause you to lose your grip on the bar when your body weight hits bottom. After you have come to a dead hang, do a plié to the ground.

In doing the bird's nest, some gymnasts muscle up, even bending their arms, but unless you can do this with control and some degree of relaxation, it is far better to just swing up and gain a sense of economy of movement. A general rule on the trapeze is to swing up and muscle down. There is a strong but mistaken tendency to do just the opposite.

Catcher's lock

This is the position assumed by the catcher in a flying return act. It is the safest way I know of hanging upside down because it is the hang used to take the weight of another person. It is certainly more secure than a single or double toe, heel, ankle or knee hang.

Whereas your hands are at least shoulder-width apart in the bird's nest, here they should be together in the center of the bar. Swing your legs the same way you did in the bird's nest, beating back (photo 8.3a) and forward (photo 8.3b). Contract the stomach muscles as if you were going to bring your knees to your chest. Instead of bending your knees to your chest and bringing your legs under the bar, however, keep your legs straight and bring them up on the other side of the bar. This time you must hook both feet right away, one on each cable (photo 8.3c). Then slide your legs straight up. They go wider and wider as you pull your pelvis right

up to the bar (photo 8.3d). You then bend your knees so that your calves wrap outside and around the cables. Your legs should be bent in such a way that your feet are no further from each other than the distance between your knees. The feet should be pointed. The bar is across the front of your thighs (photo 8.3e). Let go of the bar and hang by your knees from the cables (photo 8.3f).

To get out of the catcher's lock, you reach back up and grab the bar. If you notice where your thighs are, you will realize that the center of the bar was the only available space for your hands all along. Let your hips sag so that you do not roll over the bar. Before your legs become disengaged from the cables, pull on the bar as in an isometric exercise. This way you can gradually transfer your weight back to your arms. It will not be a sudden shock. You then do the usual plié to the ground.

Advanced trapeze hangs

The bird's nest and catcher's lock are the two basic hangs out of which come a whole range of possibilities. Perhaps the most interesting possibility of all is simply for two people to combine a catcher's lock with a bird's nest. One of them does a catcher's lock and the other does a bird's nest suspended from the arms of his partner. Ideally, one of the two partners would be familiar with both positions when the other is doing this for the first time. I usually begin by doing a catcher's lock and taking each student in my class individually in a bird's nest.

PHOTO 8.3a

PHOTO 8 3b

PHOTO 8 3d

PHOTO 8 3c

PHOTO 8 3e

PHOTO 8.3f

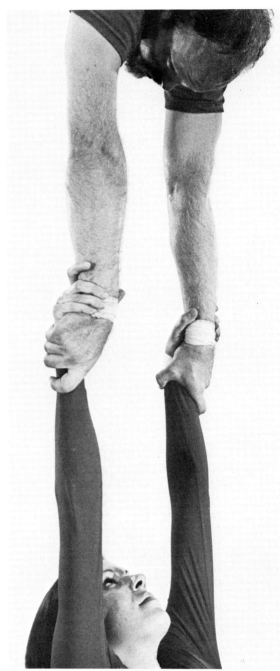

The catcher must be able to do a very good catcher's lock. He should hang limply from his knees without arching, curving or otherwise tensing his back. He should be very relaxed between his hands and knees, particularly in the shoulders and lower back. These muscles, if contracted, may not be strong enough to lift or hold people: they must be stretched and relaxed. The whole body takes the other person's weight. The only tension should be in the hands and knees.

The bottom person stands facing the catcher's upside-down face and grasps his wrists. In the proper grip, each hand is holding the partner's wrist in an interlocking wrist grip (photo 8.4); hand-to-hand would not be nearly strong enough. The bottom person should also be careful to engage the catcher's hands in a flat position rather than supinating them, as this would place the catcher's arms in a weaker position. She then kicks straight up and brings her knees to her chest and then goes into the bird's nest position (photo 8.5).

Be sure to keep your knees together when going into the position. Your knees will go between, not outside or around, the arms. Once in the position, however, push slightly apart with the feet as a precaution against becoming unhooked. Come out of the position more cautiously than you would from the bird's nest on the bar if you are very close to the floor.

If done correctly, this is a very good stretch, and certainly more of a stretch than you could give yourself on the trapeze. Weight is a factor, but not a large one as long as both people are relaxed. You can take

PHOTO 8.4

PHOTO 8.5

126 Circus techniques

someone your own weight and probably someone heavier (photo 8.6).

Another possibility growing out of the bird's nest and the catcher's lock involves one person taking certain elements from each trick and combining them to create a new trick—the ankle hang. Grasp the bar as if you were going to do a catcher's lock (hands together) and then swing your legs up and hook your feet as if you were going to do a bird's nest (feet flexed and parallel to each other, legs outside your arms). This will put you in a position (photo 8.7a) to let go of the bar, slowly straighten your legs (photo 8.7b), and hang by your ankles (photo 8.7c). Keep your feet completely flexed throughout this trick: Your life depends on it.

To slide from a knee hang to an ankle hang, grasp the bar with your hands together and hook your feet as far apart as possible over the bar. Keep your knees and feet flexed as you take your hands away and hang down (photo 8.8a). Keeping your feet flexed, push them apart as you straighten your legs (photo 8.8b) so that your feet catch on the cables (photo 8.8c). Use a mechanic when you try this or have two spotters. The spotters should stand on each side of you and each spotter should hold one of your wrists in an interlocking wrist grip and place the other hand under your shoulder.

Buster Keaton does an ankle hang in *Spite Marriage* (M-G-M Distributing Corporation, 1929), his last silent film. He is up in the rigging of a ship sitting on a boatswain's chair when he suddenly loses his balance and drops into an ankle hang.

An ankle hang on a single cable is done by hooking one ankle in the usual manner

PHOTO 8.7a

PHOTO 8.7b

PHOTO 8.6

Rigging equilibristics 127

PHOTO 8.7c

PHOTO 8.8a

PHOTO 8.8c

PHOTO 8.8b

128 Circus techniques

(photo 8.9a) but then hooking the other ankle over it in the opposite direction (photo 8.9b). You then take your hands away (photo 8.9c).

It is possible to do a bird's nest in which you are holding with one foot on one side and the opposite hand on the other side. This is a nest with only one hand and one foot. You get into it as if you were going to do a regular bird's nest, but before you take your hips through your arms, remove a hand from one side and a foot from the other side (photo 8.10). Important: Do not remove a hand and foot from the same side—it will not hold. Either right hand and left leg, or vice versa.

The one-arm and one-leg nest can also be done in the arms of a catcher. First the bottom person does a bird's nest. The catcher then releases one of her wrists, but leaves his hand there, closing the angle of his wrist so that her flexed foot and ankle form an interlocking hook with his hand and forearm. She then unhooks her other foot (photo 8.11). Getting into this position may be easy, but getting out of it can be tricky. The catcher pulls her up as he lets go of her foot and reaches for her wrist. She must overreach toward his shoulder in order to catch his wrist. Despite having just been pulled up, she is falling away from the catcher during the switch from foot to wrist.

To do a stride split under the bar, begin as if you were going to do a bird's nest but take only one leg under the bar. You then balance and do a split in that position (photo 8.12). You should also do this with the other leg. Compare this to the headstand stride split in chapter two (photos 2.6 and 2.7).

To "skin the cat," you do the beginnings of

PHOTO 8.9a

PHOTO 8.9b

PHOTO 8.9c

PHOTO 8 10

PHOTO 8 11

PHOTO 8 12

PHOTO 8.13a

PHOTO 8.13b

PHOTO 8.13c

a bird's nest, but instead of hooking your feet, you slowly bring them down over your head (photo 8.13a). From there you could go back the way you came or you could add the monkey hang. For this you must have flexible shoulders and a strong grip. Hold onto the bar very firmly with one hand and release the other hand (photo 8.13b). Because your arms were, in effect, twisted behind your back in the skin the cat, your body will now rotate 360° as it unwinds from your arm (photo 8.13c). On completion of the rotation you re-grip the bar.

Another way to vary the bird's nest is to do it hanging from the trapeze cables. You first have to go from a hang to a knee hang, to sitting on the bar, to standing on the bar. From there you grasp the cables at about shoulder height and pull your legs up into a bird's nest, hooking your feet on the cables just above your hands (photo 8.14). As you come out of it, extend your arms and lower yourself to a sitting position on the bar.

Yet another permutation would be to construct a vertical chain of three people. Before we can attempt a three-person hang we must introduce the two-person hang. The first link in the two-person hang is the catcher's lock. The second is the middle-person hang. Pulling his knees to his chest, the middle person goes to an inverted position in the hands of the catcher using the interlocking wrist grip. His center of gravity is in a relatively neutral position, from which he could continue into a bird's nest or skin the cat. Instead, they both flex their arms and the middle person's legs are pulled up through the arms and past the

PHOTO 8.14

front of the catcher's chest. The legs then come around to the small of the catcher's back, where they are locked together around the catcher's torso. They both have to be pulling together in order to get him up there. Without really moving his arms, the catcher then releases the wrists of the middle person and locks his arms around the middle person's thighs. The middle person hangs down from the catcher in a position that is similar to the catcher's lock (photo 8.15). The middle person can then take a third person in a bird's nest, completing the three-person hang (photo 8.16).

There are some things that are impossible to do on a trapeze. You cannot slide from a catcher's lock into an ankle hang. You cannot do a one-ankle hang. You do not point your toes in an ankle hang. Do not take your hands away during a bird's nest as you would for a catcher's lock. I have seen people do all of these things, and more, but fortunately I was there to catch them before they landed on their heads. It is not particularly wise to experiment up there.

Rigger's hang

The rigger's hang can also be mentioned here. It is used by circus riggers to hang from a crane bar. One leg is bent over the bar in a single knee hang position (photo 8.17a). The other leg comes around the other side of the bar, hooks over the first leg and then goes under the bar (photo 8.17b). The rigger can then hang there with both hands free and work on the rigging.

PHOTO 8.15

PHOTO 8.16

PHOTO 8 17a

PHOTO 8 17b

Variations on the trapeze

If I could have only one piece of rigging, it would be a utility trapeze. You could put hand loops on the cables and do all of your web tricks there. You can do some of the same tricks on a trapeze that are done on the horizontal bar. You can even lie out flat on it by stretching the ropes out to the side like a slack wire. Roman rings are really nothing more than two abstracted trapezes. If you take the bar off and bend it into a circle, and then bend another bar into a circle, and then hang each one from a cable, you have a pair of rings, which are not all that different from a trapeze. Basically you need segments of horizontal bar to hang from. If it is a fixed bar, then it is the equivalent of a horizontal bar. If it is not fixed, then you either have a suspended bar, two circles (rings) or some form of triangulation—or any other shape, for that matter. All you need is something to hold onto. When you come up with something new, in all probability you have complicated, not simplified, things.

Rings

Rings are included in competitive gymnastics, but there they have to be a certain height off the ground as well as a specific distance apart, and they must not move. In the circus, they are known as Roman rings and may of course be any height off the ground; they can move, but they are not used to swing on as much as they used to be. In gymnastics, rings are only a man's event, which again is not the case in the circus, where there are no such restrictions.

Rings are basically fixed points, so what you are doing is isolating your own body. Once you have mastered the trapeze, you can progress to rings rather easily, but you will not find rings as comfortable because their curvature tends to bend your fingers back. Many tricks that are performed on the trapeze can also be done on the rings, but there are some tricks that can only be done on the trapeze or only be done on rings.

The bird's nest can be done in a number of ways on the rings. The simplest and probably the best way is to hook the feet on the rings and then go through (photo 8.18). You can also do an inverted split or a knee hang from the rings, and you can sit on them with one leg through each ring. Skin the cat and the monkey hang can be performed just as easily on the rings as on the trapeze.

Some trapeze tricks would be difficult, if not impossible, on the rings, such as the ankle hang or the catcher's lock, but there are some tricks that can only be done on the rings. For example, you could do a split with one foot in each ring, either holding on or not holding on to the cables. At Muscle Beach, they do dismounts from the flying rings, up to and including a quadruple-somersault dismount, landing in the sand.

Aerial cradle

This is very similar to the trapeze. It can take many forms, but it usually consists of two

PHOTO 8.18

bars parallel to each other rather than the single trapeze bar. In Eastern Europe, the aerial cradle is often used for catching in a flying act in place of the catch trap. The catcher does a knee hang over the first bar and then hooks his flexed feet under each of two perpendicular struts or under a single, parallel second bar. In a catcher's lock, you must keep your knees bent as much as possible, whereas in the cradle you are actually pushing up with your feet. One peculiarity of the cradle is that you can drop into position in one movement, whereas to drop into a catcher's lock, you have to grasp the bar, unwrap your legs, and then rewrap them around the cables.

A cradle can be fixed or swinging and the cable can be free or rigid. You can have cradles parallel end to end or you can have them in a series. They can be used over a trampoline or in conjunction with a horizontal bar, or right above the ground. In almost all cases, it involves casting, which is a form of catapult vaulting and therefore covered in chapter nine.

Web

The web is similar to the cables of the trapeze. It is a single cable attached at a single point. The web has been relegated to the "aerial ballet" and has consequently lost whatever intrinsic interest it may have had. Plain webs are just flat webbing, but the Spanish web is round and has a hollow core with unbraided cotton rope going through it, as well as hand and foot loops attached to it.

Cloud swing

The cloud swing is constructed like a web, but is similar in configuration to a slack rope. Basically it is a glorified swing attached at both ends to a crane bar. Its shape becomes triangular when someone is on it. The cloud swing usually has hand loops attached to it, but the "Mexican cloud swing" does not and is little more than a bare slack rope. Tricks are more difficult on the Mexican cloud swing. There is also something called a cloud walk. This is a series of foot loops hung from a crane bar. The performer walks across them upside down, stepping on his instep with his foot very flexed.

Ladders

A ladder can be abstracted into a trapeze. Many tricks done on the bar and cables of the trapeze can also be done on the rungs and cables or stiles of a ladder. The swinging ladder is usually made of wood or metal and is hung from ropes that are suspended on each side at approximately 45° angles. The balancing ladder can be very dangerous and difficult if it is not locked in. It is balanced over a one-inch o.d. pipe and there is a semi-circular notch in the ladder to fit over the pipe. One person gets on each end of the ladder and they move back and forth, tilting it up and down, hopefully without upsetting the balance.

In *Cops* (First National, 1922), Buster Keaton is being chased by the police and uses a large ladder to climb over a wooden fence. Discovering more police on the other side of the fence, he reinvents the balancing ladder, causing it to balance horizontally across the top of the fence. There follows an elaborate display of weight shifting, including a back roll on the ladder, as Keaton tries to deal with the weight of the cops climbing up on each end.

The revolving ladder is similar, except it is locked in and is on bearings, so it can go all the way around. Sometimes it is first used as a balancing ladder and then whirled around, but that defeats the premise that it was, in fact, a balancing ladder. To go around, the two performers pump just like you would if you were sitting on a swing: They pull up against the ladder as they go over the top. The revolving ladder could also be missing all but the bottom rung on one side, so that one performer is treating it like a revolving ladder and the other like a trapeze, forcing out as he reaches the top so as to get over. The giant whirl can be seen as half of a revolving ladder. It is on bearings and the whole thing is a rigid frame so that it does not buckle as it goes over the top. The performer secures his feet in boots with studs on them, places his hands in hand loops with keepers over them and holds on to the sides. He then swings over the top, but there is really nothing to it. I saw Dola Sanchéz do this with just a crane bar. She simply held the ropes, put her feet in, and went around. The only things holding her up were the studs in her shoes.

Balancing trapeze

The balancing trapeze serves as a transition between gymnastic and funambulistic rigging because it is a prime example of gymnastic rigging being used for funambulistic activities. Rather than a hollow pipe 24 inches (60.96 cm.) long, the bar for the balancing trapeze is at least 30 inches (76.2 cm.) long, one inch (2.54 cm.) outside diameter, with a solid ball of steel at each end, and metal coming up each side. These metal arms are usually fixed to the bar. The trapeze end is very heavy and the cables are fairly light, which tends to make it more stable.

The most basic trick is to stand on it and take your hands away. The same thing can be done swinging back and forth, swinging sideways or swinging in a circle. A free headstand (chapter two) is in some ways easier on the balancing trapeze because it gives you an excuse for dropping your arms below your base of support. It is usually done facing one of the cables, with one leg out to each side, and a grommet is used to support the head. You can also support someone below you while doing a free headstand, but that only tends to stabilize you on the trapeze because it lowers the whole center of gravity. Another variation is to have the trapeze cables all wound up and then maintain a spinning headstand as it unwinds.

Slack rope

The slack rope is generally believed to be more difficult than the tightrope, but I do not find it so because it is so similar to balancing on the rola-bola and the unicycle. You are doing very much the same thing. Your center of gravity stays fixed while the rope sways back and forth underneath you. You are focusing on a fixed point and relating to it with your body. The only difference is that you usually balance on a slack rope with one leg and hold the other leg out so as to help your balance (photo 8.19).

Classically, you should begin by grasping the rope, going into a front rest on the rope, followed by a knee balance, and then placing the feet on the rope one at a time. This can be very difficult if you have no idea of how to walk on it.

When you are first learning, you may find it advantageous to rig the rope so its lowest point is just a few inches off the ground, and then step directly on to the rope from the ground. My own somewhat unorthodox approach has always been to place a step ladder near the middle of the rope so that the rungs are parallel to the rope. The slack rope is rigged to a height equal to that of the lowest step of the ladder. The base of the ladder nearest to the rope is placed down on the point at which the angle from the base to the first rung will be equal to the angle from the base to the rope.

To mount the slack rope, I place one foot lengthwise along the bottom rung and hold the ladder with the same hand. I place my other foot along the rope and at the same time tip the ladder toward me so that it is supported only on the base nearest the rope. When the near side of the ladder is perpendicular to the ground, my body is usually perpendicular over the rope. As soon as I feel I have my balance over the rope, I simply open my hand and the ladder tips back on all fours, making a little hop away from the rope that puts it out of my way.

I stand on one leg and use my arms and other leg to balance there. This is the best position for juggling on the slack rope. To move forward, I slide one foot forward at a time or put one foot directly in front of the other, alternately lifting each foot off the rope. Either of these movements can also be used to go backwards. When I feel I have good balance, I take longer steps. To turn around, my heels come off the rope and I quickly pivot on the balls of my feet.

The rope will have a lot of slack in the middle, but the closer you get to the end, the more it becomes like a tightrope. It will be slacking off behind you, but that does not seem to make much difference. It is never parabolic when you are on it, but instead forms two sides of a triangle, with the angles changing as you walk on it. You will probably find that the forward movement of your walk can serve to negate any swaying from side to side.

The slack rope is somewhat like a bow string, so that if you are off balance or your foot slides off, it can throw you further than would a tightrope. You are more likely to fall into a tightrope than to be thrown by it. The slack rope can also swing out from under you, but these are really the only dangers. If you can do both tightrope and slack rope, and know the difference, each one will make you better with the other. Finally, you should wear leather soles with no heel; rubber is not good.

Tightrope

The tightrope is a unique experience. There is nothing quite like it in the circus. It is easy to get hooked on the tightrope, and it is often the case that wire walkers are exclusively wire walkers. Simply to walk on a tightrope can be a very exhilarating experience because it means you know where your center is. It is very mathematical: You want half your weight falling one way and half the other: *equi-librium* (photo 8.20).

Although a properly rigged tightrope is subjected to considerable tension, you can still feel a certain lift as you walk, and this is one of the reasons it is so exciting. A gymnastic balance beam does not have the same feeling because, in addition to its greater width, it is too thick to give appreciably. You have to be on a tightrope to be doing tightrope walking. Anything else, such as walking on the edge of a fence, is simply not the same thing. The tightrope is a rope, and unless you come underneath it with trestles, it will produce a vertical oscillation that lifts your foot off the rope. It is a real thrill if you can time it so that the up-and-down vibration of the rope matches your gait and walk.

There are no rules for the placement of the feet on the tightrope. Lengthwise is fine, but I prefer a slight turnout. The more turnout, the less contact you will have with the rope, but the less likely you are to lose the support laterally. This is good for running, where you need the turnout more than the contact. On the other hand, if you were walking slowly or standing still, you might use a lengthwise step

so as to spread the support of your weight across the entire foot. A pigeon-toed walk might prevent you from falling with the rope between your legs, but I circumvent this danger by rigging the rope no higher than inseam level. You can always build up the height as you would with stilts. The only exception might arise if you were committed to a professional career. You could ruin yourself for high wire if you started low because you might develop a psychological block about going higher.

In order to maintain the balance required to walk a tightrope, you must always focus on the end of the rope. There is a tendency to look at your feet because you are so amazed that you are actually balancing there. When you turn, you have to turn a full 180° and quickly spot the other end of the rope. If you are facing sideways on the rope, you cannot see the end of the rope, which is what makes this position so very difficult and dangerous. Even when a funambulist dances on the rope, he is usually looking at one end of it. The one notable exception to this rule is Philippe Petit, who can walk across the high wire with his eyes focused on a pole he is balancing on his forehead.

PHOTO 8.19

PHOTO 8.20

9

Catapult vaulting

In catapult vaulting, the performer uses some external means of being thrown through the air. This may be animate (risley), inanimate (springboard) or a combination of both (teeterboard). The most well known examples of catapult vaulting are the trampoline and the flying trapeze.

Catapult vaulting often incorporates many of the techniques discussed in chapter six (tumble vaulting) and some of the equipment covered in chapter eight (rigging equilibristics). The catapult is usually some kind of spring or swing mechanism, but the most organic form would be one person throwing another person into the air. This category could even include super-mechanized machinery, such as a motorcycle going off a ramp and turning a somersault in the air. Almost symbolic of the circus is a person being shot out of a cannon; as early as April 22, 1879, a patent (U.S. patent no. 214,663) for such a device was issued to William Leonard Hunt. The possibilities are infinite because they can incorporate an unlimited range of hardware, software and human resources.

The fact that audiences are generally more impressed if a trick is performed off the ground, no matter how many mechanical devices are used, can lead to the use of equipment as a crutch. The subtleties of tumbling have not always been appreciated, and so ground tumbling has not remained a standard circus act. The result is that most circus acrobats do not devote themselves to pure tumbling. Since some of the best circus tumblers do specialize in catapult vaulting, it manages to produce some of the finest and most exciting circus.

Most catapults enable you to execute more turns because, the higher you go, the more time you have to somersault and twist. Any time you harness a lever or a machine to throw your body through the air, however, you had best know what you are doing. It would be foolhardy to attempt these advanced techniques without knowing the limitations of your own body. If you insist on being foolhardy, then why bother reading this book when you could be out killing yourself? Accidents do not just happen, there are usually logical reasons for them. During the pit trampoline craze of the early sixties, some people were very badly injured because they lacked the background for this kind of work and were unaware of the need for it. Even if there are no mechanical malfunctions, your own miscalculations will be magnified, and what would have been a skinned knee in tumble vaulting could here easily result in permanent injury or death. In rapid transportation, crashes and collisions lead to the inadvertent catapulting of people and a high fatality rate.

If you choose to pursue catapult vaulting, you should find committed partners as well as an experienced teacher. In addition to those tricks that do require more than one person, it is helpful to have responsible people around who know how to put up and take down the complicated rigging, can spot on a mechanic and can tell you what your body is doing.

Perhaps the following story will best illustrate the sense of blindness and dependence that typifies this work. Peg Hannah, who did a flying trapeze act with the Florida State University Circus, performed a double somer-sault dismount from the fly bar. During one performance, between the time she left the fly bar and hit the net, all the lights went out due to a power failure. She was accustomed to breaking out of her somersault based on something she could see. But when the lights went out, several voices (from the catch trap, pedestal board and ground) could be heard yelling "Break!" at exactly the same time. Normally no more than one person, if any at all, would have been calling her out of the trick.

Springboard

The springboard is perhaps the most basic catapulting device. The board bends when it is jumped on and then springs back up, catapulting the person into the air. In his *Trois Dialogues* (1599), the earliest known work on vaulting, Arcangelo Tuccaro describes a back somersault from a board placed against a wall at a 45° angle. The springboard may have developed from this early concept, perhaps as a means of doing the same thing with a front somersault.

A springboard converts forward motion into upward motion. You get the rebound plus whatever additional jump you can then add to that. No matter how high you can jump, with a catapult and proper timing you can jump even higher. In fact, timing is the most important single factor in this area.

The first exercise is simply to use the springboard to make a vertical jump. From a running approach, take off from one foot (photo 9.1a). You then hit the end of the springboard with *both* feet at the same time (photo 9.1b). The more you make the

PHOTO 9.1a

PHOTO 9.1b

PHOTO 9.1c

PHOTO 9.1d

springboard give, the greater will be the rebound effect and the higher you will go (photo 9.1c). You should land on mats or, better yet, on a crash pad. You should of course plié as you land (photo 9.1d).

Remember that the purpose of the springboard is to convert forward momentum into upward motion. You must be careful not to kill your jump by bending your knees too much as you hit the springboard, because then you will absorb the spring and not go very high at all. Once you are comfortable simply jumping from the springboard, you might try combining this with other vertical vaulting (chapter three), such as jumping off in a split, tuck, arch or other positions or jumping through a rope or hoop held in your hands. Eventually you may want to combine this with tumble vaulting (chapter six), beginning with partial and full pirouettes and going on to tiger leaps and somersaults.

Fly bar

Most people are familiar with the flying return act in which the leaper is catapulted from a fly bar into the arms of a catcher. Jules Lèotard, who invented the flying trapeze in 1859, leaped from bar to bar. Since then, all kinds of variations have been developed.

The most basic exercise is learning how to build a swing while hanging from a fly bar and how to dismount at the exact moment at the front or back of your swing. You can easily get a swing going by starting at a high point on the trapeze's pendular arc, such as from a tower or pedestal board. It is of course far more work to build a swing from a dead hang. The process is similar to pumping while sitting or standing on a playground swing. When you are going forward on the swing, you thrust your legs forward and your chest back. When you swing backwards, you put your legs back and your chest forward. You use the same method to build a swing while sitting or standing on a trapeze.

A swing can be built up in pretty much the same way when you are hanging from a fly bar, but it takes a good sense of timing and considerably more work. At the back of the swing, you sit back with your pelvis and hold your legs up in a piked position (photo 9.2a). You can then take a beat at the center by dropping your legs (photo 9.2b). As you reach the front of your swing, you force out by first raising your feet (photo 9.2c), then your legs (photo 9.2d), followed by your hips (photo 9.2e) and chest (photo 9.2f). This is an undulating movement that takes you from a piked to an arched position.

Timing plays a far greater role in achieving a high swing than does strength. It was Galileo who discovered the isochrony of pendulums: the fact that the time of a pendulum's swing depends only on its length. If it should begin to travel faster in terms of feet (meters) per second, the only way a pendulum of a given length can maintain its given oscillations per second is to swing higher. This is precisely what the sit back, beat and force out compel the pendulum (trapeze + performer) to do. If you get the timing right, it is amazing how quickly you can build a high swing.

PHOTO 9.2a

PHOTO 9.2b

PHOTO 9.2c

PHOTO 9.2d

PHOTO 9.2e

PHOTO 9.2f

If the trapeze is not too high off the ground, you can learn how to drop from the fly bar on to a mat while still swinging. Dismounts from the fly bar should be done at the moment of apparent weightlessness at the front or back of the swing. These moments when you are neither swinging forward nor backward are analogous to the moment when a juggling ball is neither traveling up nor down. To land on your feet, it is preferable to drop off the back end because you can then more easily get your feet under you. It is simply a matter of determining that precise neutral moment (photo 9.3a), releasing the fly bar, dropping vertically to the mat (photo 9.3b) and landing on your feet in a plié. Use a small amount of swing the first time you do this. If you let go too soon, you will be thrown backward; if you let go too late, you will be thrown forward. Once you can consistently find the correct moment for dropping off, you might try different variations, such as dismounting with a half-pirouette.

Voltige

Vaulting catapults can be divided into springs (e.g., the springboard) and swings (e.g., the fly bar), but it is also possible to throw a person into the air without the aid of a mechanical catapult. This kind of catapulting is called voltige. Those being thrown are known as voltigeurs while those who do the throwing are variously called the cavalier, pitcher, swinger or thrower. The form of voltige analogous to the springboard is the lift or pitch and the form analogous to the fly bar is the swing.

PHOTO 9.3a

PHOTO 9.3b

In the simplest kind of lift, the voltigeuse uses an additional thrust provided by a cavalier to jump higher than she otherwise could. The cavalier stands behind the voltigeuse, placing his hands on her waist just above the hips while she grasps his wrists. Both partners plié (photo 9.4a) and then the voltigeuse jumps as high as possible while the cavalier straightens his legs (photo 9.4b) and then his arms (photo 9.4c), transferring his upward force into the voltigeuse's leap (photo 9.4d). The timing is very important. If the voltigeuse fails to jump, she will not get very high. If the cavalier fails to plié, straighten and lift with his arms, he will not be contributing to the voltigeuse's jump. Both parts are essential and they must be done simultaneously. The cavalier must be careful not to dig his thumbs into the voltigeuse's back. In my classes, I use this lift to get students up to the trapeze if they cannot reach it themselves. In this case they would not grab my wrists because their arms would be stretched up toward the trapeze.

Although the distinction between a lift and a pitch is not all that substantial, greater elevation can be obtained by using the following basic pitch. Facing the voltigeuse, the pitcher goes into a plié, cups one hand in the other without interlocking the fingers, and holds his hands down at arm's length (photo 9.5a). The voltigeuse places one foot on the pitcher's hands and both her hands on his shoulders. The voltigeuse's raised leg will naturally be bent at the knee (photo 9.5b). The voltigeuse then jumps straight up by stretching out and pushing off her raised leg as the pitcher straightens from his plié and pushes up with

PHOTO 9.4a

PHOTO 9.4b

PHOTO 9.4c

PHOTO 9.4d

PHOTO 9.5a

PHOTO 9.5b

PHOTO 9.5c

his cupped hands. This should send the voltigeuse straight up (photo 9.5c). The two movements must be well timed. The most basic form of this is to simply go straight up and come back down, landing in a plié on a mat. It can also be used to leap over the pitcher or to do an assisted aerial back somersault.

One person can swing another in a continuous horizontal and circular arc. The voltigeuse lies face down on a mat and the swinger takes her right hand in his, using an interlocking wrist grip; he then hooks his left hand around her right foot. These are the same grips that are used for the one-arm and one-leg nest in the arms of a catcher (photo 8.11) in chapter eight, except that the arm and leg being grasped are on the same side, rather than on opposite sides of the body. The voltigeuse arches, raising her head and her left arm and leg. The swinger lifts slightly and begins pivoting in place. He does not bend forward at the waist, but instead leans back with his hips forward.

When the centrifugal force exceeds the force of gravity, the voltigeuse will swing above the floor supported only on one side (photo 9.6). By slowing down gradually, it is possible to gently return the voltigeuse to the mat. This should also be done in the opposite direction using the opposite hand and foot. It can also be done with the voltigeuse in a face-up position.

More practical than the preceding and less apt to make the participants dizzy is to use two swingers, one supporting the voltigeuse on each side. The swingers face each other and the voltigeuse is between them with her

PHOTO 9.6

back to the ground. Each swinger grasps one wrist and one ankle. Use the interlocking wrist grip for the hand and the interlocking foot hook for the ankle; the hand comes inside and under the leg. When combining the strength and effort of three people to generate catapulting force, the bare hand-to-wrist interlocking wrist grip may be weakened by perspiration. This can be counteracted by the use of wrist wraps (cotton twill tape or athletic training tape), gymnastic chalk (magnesium carbonate) and/or rosin. It is never incorrect to use these when doing any circus technique.

It is possible to begin the swing with the voltigeuse on the ground, in which case the swingers would lift her up and begin swinging. However, there is an easier and more theatrical method. The voltigeuse stands between them and the swingers grasp her wrists (photo 9.7a). One of the swingers says "hup," and on that signal she swings both of her legs up and apart at the same time. They then reach inside and grab the legs in the correct position (photo 9.7b). If her legs are together, the swingers will not be able to grab her ankles.

The swingers should lean back with their hips thrust forward so that they counterbalance each other. The voltigeuse should bend freely at the shoulders and hips. She should be careful not to round her back, however, or she may scrape the floor during her swing. She must also never throw her head back when being swung face up. She should keep her chin tucked to her chest at the center of each and every swing, no matter which direction she is swinging.

The voltigeuse can help the swingers build the swing by pumping. This is a matter of piking at the front of the swing (photo 9.7c) and then straightening the body and arching at the back (photo 9.7d). This will have quite a different effect than just limply hanging there.

The dismount must take place on a mutually agreed upon swing (photo 9.7e). The swingers release the ankles of the voltigeuse precisely at the highest point of her swing backwards (photo 9.7f). All three plié in unison, giving the voltigeuse the smoothest possible landing. If the swingers release her ankles before that neutral moment, her legs will be thrown back and out from under her. If the swingers retain their grip past the neutral moment, she will not have enough time to get her legs under her body.

The swingers must work together in order to create a smooth swing. They must have a very clear system of communicating what is going to be happening on a given swing or at a given moment. They must also be sure to lean away from each other, particularly at the bottom of each swing or otherwise the voltigeuse's back could brush against the floor.

This basic swing could be used to throw the voltigeuse a few inches into the hands of a catcher or, eventually, to throw her much greater distances, as in a quartet adagio act. It is also possible for the voltigeuse to execute twisting and turning tricks while in the air, landing on a crash pad or in the hands of a catcher.

The simplest variation on this basic swing might be to swing the voltigeuse up to a standing position on the forearms of the swingers. On a predetermined swing that is

PHOTO 9.7a

PHOTO 9.7b

PHOTO 9.7c

PHOTO 9.7e

PHOTO 9.7d

PHOTO 9.7f

high, smooth and controlled (photo 9.8a), the swingers take the voltigeuse all the way back but this time she does not arch. They swing her up between them to the highest point possible, still holding her wrists. Without letting go of the ankle, they swing their forearms away from the ankle and to a position under her foot (photo 9.8b). This must be accomplished by the time she reaches the peak of her swing backward. The swingers' elbows are braced against their hips to give the voltigeuse maximum support, while her arms are at her side (photo 9.8c).

Jacques Lecoq has defined juggling as the acrobatics of objects and acrobatics as the juggling of people. I think the various levels and types of circus techniques can provide an inspiration for new ideas. You might begin, for example, by combining voltige with the principles of the two-high (chapter five) and/or with the principles of tumble vaulting (chapter six).

Teamwork is a large factor and there is much to be gained by working with the same people on a regular basis over a long period of time. By adding more people you do not make it harder. To begin, choose the easiest two-highs and the simplest forms of tumble vaulting. With most of these skills, the best growth is made progressively. Some discoveries will be made accidentally, others by improvisation, but most will be made by hard and diligent application of known principles.

Risley

It is also possible to pitch people with your feet. The foot juggling of people is known as

PHOTO 9.8a

PHOTO 9.8b

PHOTO 9.8c

a risley act because it was said to have been originated by a circus performer by the name of Professor Risley; it is also sometimes referred to as icarianism. The top-mounter twists and/or somersaults, using the kick provided by the understander to get in and out of positions such as the seat-to-feet (photo 5.24) and feet-to-feet (photo 5.25) described in chapter five. There are of course other positions, and the top-mounter may be facing in either direction. Los Muchachos, the International Boys Circus, excels at risley.

Other springboards

The springboard's catapulting power is based on the flexibility of the wood used in its design. The trampolette, or "mini-tramp," is a variation on the springboard. The trampolette's bed is attached on all four sides to a strong frame by means of springs so that the bed gives upon impact and then rebounds. The trampolette gives more lift than most springboards, but in other respects they are quite similar.

There have been many other variations on the springboard, including the diving board used in swimming as well as a board that is attached at both ends and hit in the middle. The springboard was traditionally used in the circus in a company act in which each performer vaulted over a row of animals, usually horses or elephants. In lamenting the demise of this and other traditional company acts, Robert Sherwood wrote:

It will be observed that all these acts call for general ability among the company. Their success depends largely upon the excellence and uni-formity of training. It is precisely in this respect that the system of organization of the circus of to-day is most widely different from that of the olden time. A circus troupe is made up now largely of special performers, some of whom do brother acts, others tumbling, others bareback riding, others trapeze stunts or something else for which they have been especially trained. In everything else except the one specialty selected by them they are mediocre, even poor. Thus the troupe is made up of disintegrated parts, like a variety show.*

Teeterboard

The teeterboard resembles a seesaw in appearance and construction. One person can stand on the lower end and be catapulted into the air when his partner jumps on the high end. It is a long springboard, but instead of the support being at one end, it is in the middle. As with the springboard, you get a certain additional counterthrust. If you are on the lower end and someone jumps down on the upper end, the board itself will bend, teeter and spring because of the flexibility of the wood.

Sometimes as few as two people will work a teeterboard act. One of them runs and hits the board and then catches the other person in any one of many balance positions. However, it is more commonly used by troupes to form high human columns. The classic trick of this kind is the four-high from the teeterboard. To the best of my knowledge, a five-high has not yet been achieved on a regular

*Robert Sherwood, *Here We Are Again, Recollections of an Old Circus Clown* (Indianapolis: Bobbs-Merrill, 1926) pp.38-39

basis in performance. It has been done by using a wider base of understanders or by using a pole for support, but this is not a single-column five-high. The best teeterboard troupes have come from Hungary, Bulgaria and Moldavia.

The teeterboard is usually set in motion by someone jumping onto the upper end from a tower. The top-mounter's trajectory must be consistently precise, particularly when anything more than a two-high is being attempted. Teeterboard work should not be learned without a mechanic.

One of the most incredible circus acts I have ever seen was a back somersault on stilts from the teeterboard, which was performed by the Dovyeko troupe in the Moscow Circus. It was done with two-meter strap-on stilts, and really stopped the show. Because of the high center of gravity, the stilts made a wide sweep around the performer. The visual effect was that of a circle with the radius of the two-meter stilts. Since the troupe performed this in the United States in 1963, a somersault has also been done from the teeterboard on a single stilt, and a double somersault has been done on a pair of stilts.

Trampoline

The trampoline is probably the most popular form of springboard. It consists of a resilient canvas sheet or woven webbing supported by steel springs or shock cord springs within a metal frame. With the exception of dismounts, most trampoline tricks are performed from and to the trampoline bed, with no running start needed.

The trampoline apparently came into being as a circus act. For a brief period it was accepted in gymnastics, but is is no longer an official event. It is still used as a training tool, particularly for practicing twisting tricks, and highly organized trampoline competitions are still held regularly. Trampoline competition is scored on the basis of turns. You are allowed to hit the bed a certain number of times during your routine and you are given a certain number of points per pirouette and somersault performed within this period.

The trampoline is another example of using the height and time provided by the catapult effect in order to perform more pirouettes and somersaults. Although it can teach you how your body behaves when it is in the air, it can also be very dangerous if you lose control. You could rebound right off the trampoline bed and seriously injure yourself.

Although somersaults and pirouettes are the standard trampoline tricks, the large bed makes it possible to land in a sitting position or flat on your front or back and then bounce right back up again. This also makes the trampoline highly suited for clowning, although the clown must first be totally at home on the trampoline. The best trampoline act I ever saw was that of Larry Griswold, who also has a very good book on the subject: *Trampoline Tumbling* (New York: A. S. Barnes, 1948 and subsequent editions).

Flying trapeze

When you swing from a pendulum and then release, using that swing to catapult you, it is called casting. The familiar flying return act is usually at least thirty feet (9.14 m) off the ground, but there is also low casting. Because there is less swing and height involved, not as many turns and twists are performed while the leaper is in the air. On the other hand, a low-casting act is more suited for comedy than is a high trapeze act. Low casting is often done from bar to bar, but you can also have low casting with the catcher in a cradle. You can have casting from a horizontal bar to a catcher in a cradle, and casting can even be done over a trampoline.

All of these different casting techniques are basically just variations on the fly bar. There are infinite possibilities because methods and materials can be combined in a variety of ways. One of the best variations I have ever seen was a triple-casting act performed by the Florida State University Flying High Circus, which has always maintained a high professional standard in their casting acts. They had three cradles (chapter eight) lined up in a single lane. The leaper did a lay-out somersault to the middle catcher and then did another lay-out to the other catcher. The middle catcher became a pivotal person, as they did passing leaps and continuous lay-outs with him turning around in the middle.

A lot of people who have been trained for the flying trapeze have been excellent springboard divers: Once you are airborne, the technique is similar. Do not expect to learn these tricks from a book. You can go to a circus and observe these tricks, and there are also two interesting motion pictures that deal with the flying return and how one trains for it. *Trapeze* (United Artists, 1956), starring Burt Lancaster, is all about the triple somersault. *The Story of Three Loves* (Metro-Goldwyn-Mayer, 1953), with Kirk Douglas, shows many basic circus techniques as well as the flying trapeze. Finally, George Plimpton starred in a television special "Plimpton! The Man on the Flying Trapeze" (Wolper Productions, 1971) in which he learned a legs-across from the fly bar to the catcher.

There are a few trapeze artists who will accept a student, if the student shows promise. Many of the old-time flying return acts have broken up into old catchers with young leapers, and vice versa. The audience is rarely aware of what is going on because an experienced flyer can make a neophyte flyer look good. The really great acts have a great catcher and a great leaper. The exactitude of the timing is very important, and so they are often brothers or father and son.

Lèotard apparently invented the flying trapeze over a swimming pool. Since many tricks will be missed, it is essential to have something soft to fall into. You might fall into water, into a net, onto an air cushion, onto cardboard boxes or onto the ground. In each case, your landing will be different. If you are landing in water, you want to go in head or feet first. If you are landing on the ground, it should be feet first, followed by a deep plié and perhaps a roll. When you are falling into a net from thirty feet (9.14 m) up, you want to land on the back of your shoulders with the body somewhat tucked. The shoulders hit first, followed by the legs and head. You do not hit first with the head, arms, legs or front of the body. You can usually treat foam rubber, air cushions or cardboard boxes as a net. Cardboard boxes are great to land on because the corrugated cardboard breaks your fall when it collapses. This is the theory behind any mat, be it foam rubber, sponge rubber, kapoc or just padding. In movie stuntwork, they are always falling in the correct position for landing on the back of the shoulders, and then the camera usually cuts away at the last moment.

You can of course be seriously injured, or even killed, landing in a net. If you are not falling vertically, you could easily hit with a glancing blow and be thrown off the net. Safety laws, such as in New York State, may require wire walkers to work over a net if their high wire is above a certain height. Legislators do not realize that very few wire walkers know how to fall into a net correctly, and that this can even be terrifying to them. Flyers, on the other hand, do know how to land in a net, but if they are learning a new trick that is at all complicated, they will use a mechanic in addition to the net for safety.

If you are just swinging from the fly bar and want to drop into the net, you must do so at the neutral moment at the end of your swing. Bring your legs up to horizontal, let go of the bar, lie back with the torso and hit the net in a horizontal position with your arms out to the side. Do not grab the net. You may get a better grip on one side than on the other and be thrown right out of the net. Just bounce up and down until your bounce dies out.

Since the net is a piece of essential safety rigging, it should always be tested. In fact, the first person dropping into it from a not too difficult trick will check to be sure it is behaving right before harder tricks are attempted.

However, even a collapsing net will break your fall to a certain degree.

There are two ways of getting out of the net. Either push the spreaders apart and jump between them or grab the edges of the net and roll out. To get onto the net, you do something similar to a chin-up, except that you roll your whole body up onto it.

In modern flying return acts, the flying is from one fly bar to another person who hangs in a catcher's lock (chapter eight) from the catch trap. This person is known as the catcher, while the person who does the flying is called the leaper. There are basically three ways of catching the leaper. The most common is the interlocking wrist grip. This would be used for single, double and triple back somersaults, as well as for many other tricks. The second method uses a stick: If the leaper has his back to the catcher and does a forward somersault, his hands will be facing in the opposite direction. Since he cannot grip in this position, the catcher usually holds a stick for the leaper to grab. The third kind of catch is a legs catch. This could be used for a simple legs-across transfer but is also necessary for a single-and-a-half, double-and-a-half and triple-and-a-half back somersault because the legs come to the catcher and not the hands.

Although the usual goal is for the leaper to do as many somersaults and twists as possible before he reaches the catcher, there are many tricks in which there is hardly any turning. In a shoot-over-the-bar, for example, the leaper just rides up on the bar, dives over it and is caught. In a legs-across, the catcher simply grasps the leaper's legs as he lets go

of the bar. In the hocks-off, you are in a knee hang, whereas in the bird's nest your ankles are flexed against the bar. In either case, all you are doing is changing the shape of your body as you let go of the bar and reach out and grab the catcher. The leaper is practically caught before he lets go.

The turning and twisting tricks are basically tumble vaulting. The simplest example would be a lay-out somersault. Because of the nature of the swing, it is relatively easy for the leaper to go right into a back somersault. He just has to raise his pelvis, make only half a turn and then reach out with his arms. By the time his legs get up, he is practically there. If the trapezes are swinging to the horizontal, it is really only half of a somersault. The double somersault is a fairly standard trick, whereas the triple is one of the ultimate tricks.

A forward (somersault) over the bar uses the same approach as a shoot-over-the-bar. The leaper can also swing with his back to the catcher, release at what is actually the back of his swing, and go into a forward somersault. This is called a cutaway, and it is a stick trick because it is done facing the other way. A cutaway forward somersault with a half twist would become a hands trick again.

My favorite twisting trick is the fliffus, a double somersault with a half twist. The leaper first executes a double somersault and then looks over his shoulder. Because it is only a half twist, it becomes a stick trick; and since it is the most common stick trick, the stick used for this purpose is known as the "fliffus stick." If you go to the circus and look at the catcher's trapeze, you will often see a stick attached to the side of one of the cables. For a stick trick he unhooks it and puts it over his wrist. It is important to have a hold drilled through the stick and a piece of rope and a hand loop attached to it. There is a tremendous pull on the stick and it can roll out of your hand very easily if it rotates. Also, when the catcher is making a lock, he cannot be holding the fliffus stick and therefore it is convenient to have it hooked over his wrist.

The ultimate flying trapeze trick is the "legendary triple." Very few performers have accomplished it, and some have died trying. It is now becoming more common, and a few have done even a triple-and-a-half back somersault, which of course is a legs trick. (I have now seen the triple somersault from a fly bar, teeterboard, Russian swing and horizontal bar; I have seen a triple-and-a-half somersault from a fly bar and have heard of a quadruple somersault from the Roman rings and from a diving board.)

The closing trick in many flying return acts is the passing leap. This involves two people passing in mid-air, and there are many ways of doing it. One leaper goes across and, as he comes back, another leaper goes across. The catcher is practically in a juggling position as he releases one leaper and grabs the other. One of the most common ways of executing the passing leap is to combine a legs-across with a forward over the bar. I recall seeing a *Tarzan* movie on television in which Jane and Tarzan performed a passing leap to a "gorilla" catcher.

The role of the catcher in flying return acts is generally unappreciated, but it is of course critical and deserves a detailed explanation. The catcher has to have the right temperament for the job because the audience always gives credit to the leaper. But if you do have the right attitude and a real feeling of responsibility for the other person, it is possible to become a catcher. It is exacting work, but it is not all that difficult. The catcher does not even have to be strong, although some extra strength can help when the trick goes wrong.

The basic grip used by catcher and leaper is hands to wrists. However, you do not go directly for this hold or you will often miss it. Instead, you try to make contact way up on the arm and then slide down. It makes catching more feasible because it gives you more margin for error.

The catcher does not just instantaneously catch a trick. He must evaluate the trick and then catch it or not catch it. He does not have much time to make a decision, and yet he must make a decision. If there is anything wrong whatsoever with the timing—if the leaper is there at the wrong time, if his swing was too high, if he traveled too far or not far enough—the catcher will elect not to catch the trick. Many bad tricks are easy to take but impossible to hold onto throughout the swing. The catcher may be able to hold onto it even at center, but if the leaper and catcher are not swinging together, there is still a tremendous whip. The greatest pull is at center and not at the catch point. It is exceedingly dangerous to take a poorly timed trick, because the tangent at center is horizontal and not likely to make the leaper land in the net.

Therefore it is a question of whether the catcher can hold the leaper through the entire swing. If he takes him, he has to hold him past center. Training and performance are two different things: Flyers often go for tricks in performance that they would not go for in practice. That is why you see so many tricks with bad timing in performance. Obviously the catcher is not going to desperately grab hold of anything within reach. If the trick is missed at the catch point, it is probably the decision of the catcher, and not because he could not make physical contact. If you see the catcher lose the trick at the end of the swing or when they swing back to center, then it is probably a trick that should not have been taken.

If a trick is not caught, the leaper should continue to turn in such a way as to land on the back of his shoulders. Some leapers will twist over onto their backs by doing a half-pirouette as they fall to the net. You should never do a trick if you do not know how to make a landing out of it.

In *Our Hospitality* (Metro Pictures Corporation. 1923). Buster Keaton uses the principles of the flying trapeze to rescue his girl friend who is floating over a waterfall. Instead of being in a catcher's lock, he simply has a rope around his waist that is tied to a log. He swings out on the rope and grabs her hands just as she is coming over the edge of the waterfall. It is very much in the image of the flying trapeze. Keaton catches her by the backs of her wrists, but in the next shot their hands are in the interlocking wrist grip. Since the second "girl" was actually larger than Keaton. the first was probably a dummy and the second a stuntman.

The best methods of critical research that I have encountered are described in Alden Todd's *Finding Facts Fast* (New York: Morrow, 1972). These methods, designed to efficiently research any subject, would lead you to the key bibliographical circus reference: Raymond Toole-Stott's *Circus and Allied Arts: A World Bibliography, 1500–1970* (Derby, England: Harpur, 1958–1971). This standard work is discussed in two excellent guides to circus source material: "A Selected Guide to Source Material on the American Circus" by Richard W. Flint in the *Journal of Popular Culture* (Vol. VI, No. 3, pp. 615–619), Bowling Green University, University Hall 100, Bowling Green, Ohio 43403, and "Sources in Popular Entertainment" by John Towsen in *The Drama Review* (Vol. XVIII, No. 1, pp. 118–122), School of the Arts, New York University, 32 Washington Place, Room 74, New York, New York 10003.

The most valuable information you might learn about circus techniques could be from direct observation of circus techniques being performed. An obvious possibility is to see circuses. (The best directory of circuses is the *Carnival & Circus Booking Guide,* published annually by Amusement Business, P.O. Box 2150, Radnor, Pennsylvania 19089.) Circus routes are published in *Amusement Business,* P.O. Box 2150, Radnor, Pennsylvania 19089; *The Circus Report,* 525 Oak Street, El Cerrito, California 94530, and *Today Is Circus Day in* ———, Charlie Campbell, 150 Tenth Street, N.E., Apt. 203, Atlanta, Georgia 30309. Circus reviews and photographs are published in *Southern Sawdust,* L. Wilson Poarch, Jr., 2965 Freeman Avenue, Sarasota, Florida 33580. Photographs and articles (in Russian) on the Soviet circus are published in (#70844) *Sovetskaia Estrada i Tsirk* which is available from Four Continent Book Corporation, 149 Fifth Avenue, New York, New York 10010.

Common interest groups centering around some aspect of circus techniques have been organized and membership can be most enriching. A few are mentioned here along with their respective publications. *Acrobatics* (6, Elizabeth Way, Hanworth, Feltham, Middlesex TW13 7PH, England) is the official journal of the Association of Acrobats. The International Jugglers' Association (Carol Benge, Secretary, 129 Fourth Avenue, Bartlett, Illinois 60103) publishes the *IJA Newsletter.* The *USA Newsletter* (Bill Jenack, Editor, 67 Lion Lane, Westbury, New York 11590) is published by the Unicycling Society of America. *AcroSports* is the official publication of the United States Sports Acrobatics Federation (P.O. Box 777, Santa Monica, California 90406).

There is no single, convenient, "circus factory, supply house or store" that mass-produces and distributes all the equipment used in circus techniques. A few items are stocked, or made to order, by a few highly specialized sources. Some equipment can be easily constructed from common materials. Often specialized equipment, such as sporting goods, can be ingeniously adapted for circus use. (The best guide for locating specific sporting goods is *The Sporting Goods Directory,* published annually by The Sporting Goods Dealer, P.O. Box 56, St. Louis, Missouri 63166.) The selected glossary of materials and supplies that follows illustrates the truism that, "circus equipment is where you find it." Cross references are indicated by small capitals.

Anchors

Anchors are simply points to which tight and slack ROPES, crane BARS and other rigging can be guyed out. Outdoors screw anchors (such as those used to guy out telephone poles and house trailers in hurricane areas) will be safer

than the traditional wood or iron stakes. Indoor anchors should be attached to or through the floor or wall. The ones I use are welded to the vertical I-beams of the building structure. Where actual attachment is impractical, trucks or heavily weighted sledges may be used. A tug-of-war, that is to say human anchorage, may even provide sufficient ballast for an experienced rope-walker. See also crane BARS.

Balls, Juggling

The best balls made especially for juggling are, unfortunately, no longer available. They were made by the late Harry Moll of Denver, Colorado. There was a solid white rubber ball two and a quarter inches in diameter and also a solid yellow rubber ball one and three quarters inches in diameter.

The closest approximations to these balls are the solid, hard, rubber balls made for the sport of lacrosse and for dogs to chew and play with. Lacrosse balls are two and a half inches in diameter and come in white and orange. The indoor version is rather "dead," but the outdoor version is an excellent bouncer. They may be purchased in sporting goods stores. The dog balls come in a greater variety of diameters and colors and can be obtained from pet stores.

Bars, Crane

Crane bars are the key units from which TRAPEZES, Roman RINGS and other rigging are suspended. The crane bar, in turn, is traditionally hoisted into position by two simple manual cranes consisting of a rigging HOOK and manila rope threaded through a single pulley block attached near the top of the center poles of a circus tent. Once in position, this crane bar

should also be guyed out to ANCHORS. The indoor crane bars that I use are welded to the horizontal I-beams of the building structure and are therefore not hoisted into position nor is it necessary to guy them out. They consist of three-and-a-half-inch outside diameter steel pipes.

In order to attach rigging to the crane bars without welding to them or drilling holes in them, I use two types of collars that can be bolted tightly to the crane bar, but remain forever flexible to future adjustments. I prefer to use swing hangers which can be obtained from playground equipment supply companies. They are held in place by two bolts and have an eye hanging down that is mounted on nonlubricated bearings. If no swinging is to take place a split mast band makes a fair substitute for a swing hanger. I have only seen these for sale in marine hardware stores in San Francisco. Rigging is attached to the collars by means of rigging HOOKS, SHACKLES or CARABINERS.

Beckets

Beckets are short lengths of rope with eye splices in each end. They may be threaded through each other, interlaced in a configuration resembling a square knot and/or linked with SHACKLES to extend TRAPEZES, guy out slack ROPES, etc.

Boards, Spring

Currently required for the vaulting events in both men's and women's competitive gymnastics, springboards are readily available from numerous gymnastic supply houses. The one I use, however, was built from plans found in *Acrobatics in School* (in Russian) by A. M. Ig-

nashenko which was published in Moscow in 1964.

At one time springboards, flying rings and trapezes were common to both the circus and the swimming pool, but today the springboard is hardly ever seen in an American circus and I have never seen flying rings or trapezes at a swimming pool. The use of rings and trapezes for diving is discussed in *Swimming and Diving* prepared by the American Red Cross (Garden City, New York: Doubleday, 1938).

Carabiners

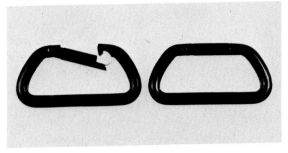

Originally designed for use in mountain climbing, carabiners have certain circus rigging applications as well: they combine the interchangeability of SHACKLES with the linking speed of rigging HOOKS. The carabiner consists of a strong, elongated, trapezoidal ring with a hinged segment along the short parallel side that opens inward. A powerful spring automatically closes this jaw unless it is held or wedged open. Carabiners are sold in outdoor sporting goods stores.

Chairs, Bentwood

Most any chair can be balanced, but the bentwood chair is my favorite because of its great strength and extreme lightness. Its construction was pioneered by Michael Thonet in

1855. Although expensive, I have been able to find all I need discarded (slightly damaged) on the sidewalks of New York City. This chair is also a favorite among lion trainers.

Chalk

Gymnastic chalk may be used to counter the negative and dangerous effect of perspiration that tends to accumulate on the hands when doing hand-to-hand or hand-to-rigging circus techniques. It is a compound chemically known as carbonate of magnesia or magnesium carbonate ($MgCO_3$). It is less dense and crumbles more easily than the more familiar calcium carbonate ($CaCO_3$) or blackboard chalk. It may be purchased in blocks weighing one or two ounces or in powdered form from sporting goods stores and gymnastic supply houses. It is usually imported from France or Italy by such companies as Glyco Chemicals, Inc., 51 Weaver Street, Greenwich, Connecticut 06830. It may be used alone or *before* applying ROSIN.

Clubs, Juggling

For half a century the best juggling clubs were made by the late Harry H. Lind of Jamestown, New York. He had customers all over the world and the clubs were made by hand of wood and cloth to his own exacting specifications. I now use one of the same Lind designs, fashioned in fiberglass by Stuart Raynolds, Scientifically Crafted Juggling Apparatus, 2716 Silverside Road, Wilmington, Delaware 19810. These clubs are an exact reproduction of the exterior Lind design, but are lighter and more durable.

Another method of making clubs seems to have been pioneered by Dave Madden, who was the first juggler I know of to make a "juggling club" out of a standard-sized plastic toy bowling pin by cutting off the bowling pin at its narrowest point and inserting a wooden handle. This method of construction was further sophisticated by Jay Green (Jerry Greenberg) and is described by Carlo (Charles Lewis) in *The Juggling Book* (New York: Random House, 1974). This type of club can be purchased from Jay Green, 1565 East 9th Street, Brooklyn, New York 11230 or Brian Dube, 7-13 Washington Square North, Apt. 47-B, New York, New York 10003.

Yet another method of making clubs is used in Eastern Europe. A handle, a plywood spreader and a base are strung along a dowel spindle and ribs of split bamboo are stretched over the spreader and attached to the handle and the base. The ribs are then covered with a "skin" such as plastic TAPE.

Cylinders, Foot Juggling

I use ordinary, cylindrical, cardboard tubes which are used as a protective core for shipping rolled up rugs or fabric. I prefer a fairly heavy cylinder about three and a half inches in diameter and five to six feet long. They could be obtained from cardboard companies or rug stores, but I find all I need discarded in the manufacturing districts of New York City. I usually seal the ends with athletic training TAPE to reduce fraying.

Diabolos

The French type of concentric, conical diabolo is fairly easy to make. I make them on a wood-turning lathe from five-inch lengths of four-by-four lumber. Another method is to remove one or both spouts from a pair of funnels which can then be bolted or soldered together. Handsticks can be made of wooden dowel or bamboo reeds about eighteen inches long and a half inch in diameter. Cotton butcher's string seems to work the best, but has to be replaced often.

In recent years I have been fortunate enough to obtain a limited number of authentic, hollow, bamboo diabolos which were imported from the People's Republic of China and sold in Chinese shops in New York and San Francisco. These are excellent and even have the traditional noise holes on the rims so that they make a loud humming or whirring sound when they are spun—the pitch varying with the speed of rotation.

Plastic diabolos for children can be purchased in toy stores. They are available in a variety of models of both the Chinese and French design.

Feathers, Peacock

Peacock feathers have become popular for feather arrangements and can often be obtained from florists.

Hooks, Rigging

Rigging hooks are long open hooks with a six-inch-deep throat, hairpin turn and welded eye in one end. They can be hooked quickly and safely. They are used extensively in circus performances where rapid rigging changes must be effected. Traditionally they are spliced to the main falls which are used in a circus tent to hoist rigging. Likewise TRAPEZES and other rigging usually terminate in rigging hooks which are used to attach them to crane BARS. They are usually made from half-inch diameter steel rod. They may be purchased from Zacchini Machine Shop, 1208 North Orange Avenue, Sarasota, Florida 33577.

Hoops

In addition to eccentric spinning, hula hoops, which are sold in toy stores, are also useful for hoop jumping à la jump ROPE and tiger leaps. I remove and discard the rattling ball bearings they sometimes contain and close the hoop back up with athletic training TAPE.

Knives, Rigging

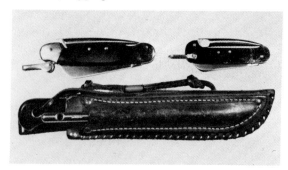

The pocket rigging (or yachtsman's) knife has a blade and a fid each of which fold into the handle. With some the fid "locks" in the open position and will not fold into the handle unless "released" first. These knives are invaluable to the rigger. The blade is designed for cutting manila and other rope. The fid is useful for opening up strands of manila rope when constructing TRAPEZES. In the course of erecting and dismantling rigging, frequent use of the fid will be made to tighten and loosen SHACKLES.

There is a smaller version of the pocket rigging knife called a sailor's knife. The advantage of this is its more convenient size. I carry a sailor's knife when I am not sure I will need a rigging knife, but when I have a lot of rigging work to do I prefer a sheath rigging knife. The sheath hangs from a belt loop and has individual pockets for the knife and fid, neither of which fold.

Rigging knives may be purchased from cutlery stores, marine hardware stores and sporting goods stores. There are many brands of pocket rigging knives, but the best I have found are the Ka-bar and the Buck.

Lariats

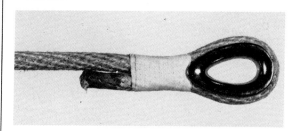

Lariats (or lassos) for rope spinning should be made from #12 braided cotton sash cord—also called spot cord. (When one of the strands is colored it produces a regular pattern of spots on the surface of the rope.) Sash cord is sold in hardware stores and an old and respected manufacturer is Sampson Cordage Works, Boston, Massachusetts 02210. The size is critical so be sure to use #12 which is three-eighths of an inch in diameter. Although #10 is easier to obtain and only one-sixteenth of an inch narrower in diameter, it is *not* suitable for rope spinning.

I use a twenty-foot length of rope for both the horizontal and vertical loops. I make a honda (eye) for the horizontal loop by doubling the rope back on itself and making a dozen or so

wraps with # 18 or # 20 copper wire followed by a few layers of athletic training TAPE. For the vertical loop, where a heavier honda is required, I use a commercially founded brass honda which is sold in western riding stores such as H. Kauffman & Sons Saddlery Co., 139 East Twenty-fourth Street, New York, New York 10010. I simply attach the honda temporarily with athletic training TAPE, although the traditional procedure is to attach it more permanently and even hammer the rim of the honda down around the rope.

Mats

I find black sponge rubber mats to be of great use: to break your fall in tumbling and dismounting from rigging, to protect juggling props and reduce noise when they are dropped, etc. I use the ordinary yard wide sponge rubber that is used under rugs and other flooring. I prefer the half-inch thickness and usually buy fifty-foot lengths which I cut into two twenty-five-foot lengths. For many purposes I will use two or three layers which increases the effective thickness. Sponge rubber is very heavy and should probably be purchased from your nearest source. United Rubber Supply Co., 54 Warren Street, New York, New York 10007 was recommended to me by the late Joe Price.

Gymnastic supply houses make special tumbling mats which are five feet wide (standard for tumbling competition). They can also furnish thick (four to eighteen inches) safety landing mats which are most advisable to use for catapult vaulting.

Mechanics

The mechanic (photo 8.1) that I use is constructed quite simply from a fifty-foot length of three-eighths of an inch diameter synthetic fiber braided rope, a single and a double three-inch pulley block, two bronze dog snaps and a tumbling belt. Note that I do not use the hooks on the pulley blocks to attach them to the crane BAR, but attach CARABINERS or SHACKLES to the *eye* of the hook. The ideal angle between the belt and either pulley block is 45°. To protect the hand of the spotter I prefer a leather truck driver's type of glove. The tumbling belt should be purchased from a gymnastic supply house (I prefer the #H-470 tumbling belt manufactured by Premier Athletic Products, 25 East Union Avenue, East Rutherford, New Jersey 07073). The other components can be purchased separately.

George Szypula's excellent *Tumbling and Balancing for All* (Dubuque, Iowa: W. C. Brown, 1957) contains further information on mechanics, both stationary and traveling as well as the Pond twisting belt (U.S. patent #2496748).

Rings, Juggling

Juggling rings are usually cut from sheets of profile material such as plastic or plywood. I use quarter-inch plywood. cut the rings to an outside diameter of from twelve to sixteen inches, and give the rims a width of one and nine-sixteenths inches. The larger diameter is preferable for eccentric spinning.

It is difficult to cut these rings freehand. The system I use is to cut the plywood into square tiles equal to the diameter I would like and drill a small hole at the center of each tile. Then fix a nail at right angles to the blade of a band saw and at a distance equal to the radius of the finished ring. Now the hole in the tile is simply dropped over the nail and the tile rotated into the teeth of the saw until a full circle

has been cut. For the center cut the radius is reduced by one and nine-sixteenth inches and the process is repeated, but using a saber saw mounted upsidedown. After cutting the inside circle halfway, I turn the tile over and recut the full circle in the opposite direction.

The ring is then smoothed with sandpaper and taped with athletic training TAPE. I then often add a reinforcing compression ring of plastic TAPE around the outside. This tape stretches into a nice channel shape, but should be overlapped at least the amount it was stretched as it tends to slowly retract.

Rings, Roman

Of the older gymnastic apparatus such as the Roman chair, Roman ladders, Roman pillar and Roman rings, only the Roman rings are frequently seen today in the form of the still rings event which continues today in men's competitive gymnastics. These may be obtained from gymnastic supply houses. I purchase only the rings themselves (rubber with a metal core or laminated wood) and splice five-eighths or three-quarter-inch diameter manila rope to them and then suspend them from a crane BAR about eighteen inches apart. These could also be used for flying rings, the technique for which is essentially the same as for the fly bar. Flying rings was an event in competitive gymnastics for men from 1885 to 1962 and for women from 1933 to 1957.

Rola-Bolas

The rola-bola board is very easily constructed using simple conventional woodworking methods. I use a board made of three-quarter-inch plywood that is thirty-two inches long and twelve inches wide. I use the best side as the

bottom (which will be in contact with the cylinder) and attach a one-inch-by-two-inch-by-twelve-inch strip of wood to each end to act as a brake. For better footing I add treading to both ends of the top surface. This could be grooved rubber treading, but I prefer 3M brand Safety-Walk (manufactured by Minnesota Mining and Manufacturing Company, St. Paul, Minnesota 55101) which can be purchased at marine and other hardware stores. I put three one-inch-wide strips, one inch apart, at each end of the board.

The rola-bola cylinder can be made by laminating four two-by-sixes together and then turning them down on a lathe to a cylinder a little less than six inches in diameter and twelve inches long. I have also used one-foot sections of aluminum pipe from four and a half to six inches in outside diameter with a quarter-inch-thick wall.

The Bongo Board (manufactured by the Bongo Corporation, 645 Madison Avenue, New York, New York 10022) may be purchased from toy, sporting goods and ski stores. The patented tongue-and-groove feature can be rendered inoperative simply by removing the tongue that runs along the underside of the board. You cannot, however, use these cylinders for double rola-bola, because the grooves in the cylinders will lock together which results in no rolling!

Ropes, Jump

An ordinary length of #10 braided cotton sash cord makes a fine jump rope. Rope can also be purchased with handles and bearings. The best quality jump rope I know of has leather rope, hardwood handles and ball bearing swivels. It is manufactured by Everlast Sporting Goods Co., 750 East One Hundred Thirty-second Street, Bronx, New York 10454. It comes in two sizes: #4496 which is eight feet long and #4497 which is nine and a half feet long. There is also the My-Jump rope, imported from Japan, which has a digital counter built into one of the handles—it counts the number of jumps you make.

Ropes, Slack and Tight

It is possible to use mostly the same components to rig both a slack rope and a tightrope. Each requires a rope, a pair of jacks, a pair of guys and a pair of ANCHORS. The tightrope is tightly guyed out; the slack rope is not.

For the rope I use a half-inch or five-eighths-inch diameter steel wire rope, but it is also possible to use a fiber rope.

The method I use for constructing jacks is the simplest and least expensive I know. Each jack is constructed of two six-foot two-by-fours, one eye bolt, one eye nut, two regular nuts and bolts, a length of strong chain and a few washers. Holes are drilled in each two-by-four at the bottom, two feet up from the bottom and near the top.

For the slack rope the jacks are assembled in an A-shape by running the eye bolt through the top holes and attaching the eye nut. The chain is bolted across the middle holes to prevent the two-by-fours from becoming any wider at the base than you wish.

For the tightrope the jacks are assembled in an X-shape by running the eye bolt through the middle holes and attaching the eye nut. The chain is bolted across the bottom holes.

To guy out the slack rope I use a series of manila rope BECKETS at one end and a (double-single) block and tackle at the other. The block and tackle are not to draw the rope tight, simply to allow me to adjust the height; beckets could be used at both ends.

To guy out the tightrope, I use a heavy anchor chain and a chain hoist (I use a 1.5 ton *Nitchi* Puller Ratchet Lever Hoist manufactured by the Nich Co., Osaka, Japan—distributed in the United States by the American Gage & Mfg. Co.).

I use SHACKLES to link all these components together. I use rope clips to make an eye in each end of the rope. It is essential that you use the right size for the rope, place three at each eye, and place the U-bolt against the free end of the rope and the saddle against the long end of the rope.

Rosin

Rosin is the dry, hard product of resin which is derived from the sticky pitch/sap of trees. It is dark amber and looks like glass, but when crushed into a fine powder it appears almost white. By dusting rigging, wrist wraps, hands and soles of the feet or shoes with powdered rosin, one's grip can be improved in a controlled way. Some people, however, are allergic to rosin (it can cause rash or infection), so caution should be used and the direct application to the bare skin discontinued for those who have a reaction to it.

Rosin can be purchased from sporting goods stores in two-ounce quantities already powdered and sewn into little cotton bags such as those prepared by Cramer Products, Inc., 153 West Warren, Gardner, Kansas

66030. It is also possible to purchase rosin in chunk form, pulverize it with a hammer and put it into refillable cotton bags with drawstrings (such as tobacco bags). The drawstring is especially useful if you want to tie the bag to rigging.

Shackles

Perhaps no other rigging component has broader or more versatile applications than the screw pin anchor shackle. It is U-shaped, somewhat bowed and has a threaded pin that bolts the opening of the jaws closed. They may be used to connect ANCHORS, split mast bands, BECKETTS, eye bolts, CARABINERS, anchor chains, swing hangers, rigging HOOKS, eye nuts, other shackles, eye splices, etc. to one another. They are made of bronze or steel (with a variety of finishes) in an enormous range of sizes, and are very strong for their size and weight. Galvanized steel is the least expensive and three sizes will cover most circus applications: half-inch (holds two tons), seven-sixteenths-inch (holds one and a half tons) and three-eighths-inch (holds one ton). When the shackle is in use the pin should be tightened. A fid such as is found on rigging KNIVES is inserted through the hole in the flattened knob of the pin and used as a lever to turn the pin (clockwise to tighten, counterclockwise to loosen). Shackles can be purchased from farm and marine hardware stores.

Sticks, Cue

Just about any old cue stick will work fine for balancing. Used, worn, damaged or warped cue sticks can often be obtained for a fraction of their usual cost. Athletic training TAPE can be attached to the tip to form a soft, textured surface that is free from dirt and traces of blue chalk.

Sticks, Devil

The long stick I use is a one-and-a-quarter-inch diameter dowel twenty-six inches long. It is tapered to an hourglass shape on a wood turning lathe. There is much latitude for personal preference where the dimensions are concerned. Generally you will find the greater the taper the better the devil stick will work, but the narrower the waist the more fragile and likely to snap in two the stick will be. Thus the designer must trade off effectiveness with durability and come to some happy compromise. The easiest way to make handsticks is simply to cut a yard long, half-inch diameter dowel into two eighteen-inch lengths (by adding string these same handsticks can also be used for DIABOLO). To improve visibility, friction and strength, I wrap all the sticks with athletic training TAPE.

Sticks, Juggling

The sticks that I use for toss juggling are made by sleeving a three-and-a-quarter-inch length of one-and-a-half-inch diameter dowel over a sixteen-and-a-quarter-inch length of one-inch diameter dowel. This is turned on a lathe so that there is a twelve-inch handle that tapers slightly to a one-inch bead, followed by a three-and-quarter-inch end. These may be purchased from Stuart Raynolds, Scientifically Crafted Juggling Apparatus, 2716 Silverside Road, Wilmington, Delaware 19810. The design is from *The Art of Juggling* (in Russian) by N. E. Bauman, a teacher at the Moscow Circus School. Published in Moscow in 1962 and translated into German in 1969, this excellent book on juggling is difficult to obtain.

Stilts

Stilts are fairly easy to make using ordinary materials and conventional woodworking methods. I usually build them from a pair of eight-foot two-by-twos. Steps can be cut from two-by-fours. I use a series of tangential circles with a diameter equal to the width of the two-by-four to geometrically construct a reverse curve (ogee) stilt step design that enables me to make a single curved cut with a band saw and get two seven-and-a-half-inch stilt steps from one nine-and-a-half-inch length of two-by-four without wasting any lumber. I usually attach the steps to the stiles with countersunk wood screws and white glue at a height of twenty-six inches and an extra pair of steps on the opposite side of each stile at a height of thirty-six inches. To attach the steps instantly and adjustably, use carriage bolts and no glue. The stilts can be made more streamlined by tapering them toward the top. To avoid

splinters sand the stiles very carefully. For indoor use the bottom end should be equipped with rubber treading to avoid slipping. I usually stretch a strip of grooved rubber treading about the width of the stile and some ten inches long (grooves running lengthwise) over the base end of the stile and fastened in place with tacks or staples. I then place a second strip perpendicular to the first and wrap both with athletic training TAPE. The treading wears through very rapidly and should be checked frequently and replaced as often as is necessary.

Stilts by S. Carl Hirsch (New York: Viking Press: 1972) is an excellent little book (primarily for children) on the history of stilt-walking which also includes information on building stilts. Stilts for children can, of course, be purchased in toy stores.

Tape, Athletic Training

Athletic training tape is a cloth tape with a mild adhesive. It is similar to, but not to be confused with, surgical adhesive tape. It is sold in sporting goods stores and there are a number of brands (Johnson & Johnson, Bike/Kendall, Arno/Dr. Scholl's, etc.). I prefer the one-and-a-half-inch width which comes eight rolls to the cardboard container. Although it is expensive, I am constantly finding new uses for it.

Tape, Cotton Twill

Wrist wraps made of cotton twill tape are a useful aid to circus techniques which use the interlocking wrist grip. They are easy to grip (especially if dusted with ROSIN), their white color makes them very visible, they support the wrist, they absorb perspiration, they are reusable and more comfortable than the adhesive athletic training TAPE.

I usually purchase Wright's brand cotton twill tape in a three-fourths-inch width from the Woolworth's variety store chain. It comes wrapped on a card in two-yard lengths—the perfect amount for one wrist. Starting at the base of the wrist and leaving about a six-inch loose end, wrap and overlap up the arm until you have used half of the material. Then wrap and overlap back down the arm to where you started. Tie the loose ends on the *back* of your wrist and use a popsicle stick to tuck the loose ends under the wraps.

Tape, Plastic

I find waterproof, stretchy Scotch brand plastic tape, which is manufactured by Minnesota Mining & Manufacturing Co., 3M Center, St. Paul, Minnesota 55101 and sold in stationery and variety stores, very useful. I use the (#190) three-quarter-inch width to reinforce plywood juggling RINGS. I use the (# 191) one-and-a-half-inch width to construct a skin between the ribs of bamboo juggling CLUBS. This tape is available in a number of bright, decorator colors.

Trampolines

While the trampoline can trace its origins to the circus, it has also enjoyed popularity as a competitive sport, recreational activity and an aid to diving, gymnastic and military training. Over half a dozen gymnastic suppliers manufacture trampolines, the oldest of which is the Nissen Trampoline Co., Cedar Rapids, Iowa 52406.

Trapezes

A good utility trapeze can be constructed from a length of plumber's pipe two feet long and one inch in *outside* diameter. (Plumbers tend to think of this as three-fourths-inch *inside* diameter with a one-eighth-inch wall.) Drill one-fourth-inch holes all the way through the pipe one-and one-half inches from each end. Take a length of three-fourths- or five-eighths-inch diameter, three-strand, twisted, manila rope (several feet longer than twice the length of the trapeze you want to make) and eye-splice each end to the ends of the pipe. As you do this open one of the strands of the rope with the fid of a rigging KNIFE. Run a one-fourth-inch carriage bolt through the strand (not between strands), through the pipe, and then through the same (or another) strand of the rope. In this way you bolt the eye splice to the bar so that it cannot slide along or *off* the bar. Add a washer and nut to the bolt. Tighten the nut. Cut off any excess bolt that protrudes past the nut more than one-fourth-inch. The bolt is now peened down over the nut—so the nut will never be able to loosen. Now you can cut the ropes to the length you want the trapeze to be, allowing enough excess to splice rigging HOOKS, or eyes, into the ends of the ropes. The cables should be padded where they meet the bar. I find strips of cloth, strips of inner tubes and athletic training TAPE useful for this purpose. Finally, upholster the padding with cloth and wrap the bar with athle-tic training tape. The trapeze is now ready to be hung from a crane BAR.

A slightly different type of trapeze bar can be purchased from the Zacchini Machine Shop, 1208 North Orange Avenue, Sarasota, Florida 33577. Instead of using a bolt to hold the eye splice in place on the bar, the splice is sewn to a perforated rim and a thick threaded weight is screwed up against it.

To make a fly bar I have one-quarter-inch steel plate welded to the ends of a solid, one-inch diameter, steel rod that is thirty-inches long. These additions are then cut into an egg shape and holes are drilled in the part protruding from the bar. Small shackles can then be used to attach the bar to BECKETS of one-eighth-inch steel *airplane* cable.

Unicycles

The finest professional unicycles were custom manufactured by the late Harry Sykes (Sykes Bikes) of Chicago, Illinois. These were often chrome-plated and many of them are still in use today. Reasonably good service can be obtained from some of the better quality recreational unicycles that are readily and inexpensively available from bicycle stores. These are manufactured domestically and imported from Japan. I prefer the Oxnaco import which is available in three models: twenty-inch regular, twenty-four-inch regular and twenty-inch high (giraffe). Many of the parts are interchangeable among these three models. Instructions for building regular, midget and high unicycles can be found in the appendices of *The Unicycle Book* by Jack Wiley (Harrisburg, Pennsylvania: Stackpole, 1973).